I0522275

Self-Love Workbook For Teens Girls

Boosting Self-Esteem, Unleashing Self-Confidence, and Unveiling the Strong and Independent Woman Within

AMORA K. ROSE

© Copyright 2023 by Amora Rose - All rights reserved.
The content contained within this book may not be reproduced, duplicated or transmitted without direct written permission from the author or the publisher.
Under no circumstances will any blame or legal responsibility be held against the publisher, or author, for any damages, reparation, or monetary loss due to the information contained within this book, either directly or indirectly.
Legal Notice:
This book is copyright protected. It is only for personal use. You cannot amend, distribute, sell, use, quote or paraphrase any part, or the content within this book, without the consent of the author or publisher.
Disclaimer Notice:
Please note the information contained within this document is for educational and entertainment purposes only. All effort has been executed to present accurate, up to date, reliable, complete information. No warranties of any kind are declared or implied. Readers acknowledge that the author is not engaged in the rendering of legal, financial, medical or professional advice. The content within this book has been derived from various sources. Please consult a licensed professional before attempting any techniques outlined in this book.
By reading this document, the reader agrees that under no circumstances is the author responsible for any losses, direct or indirect, that are incurred as a result of the use of the information contained within this document, including, but not limited to, errors, omissions, or inaccuracies.
Image by Freepik.com. This cover has been designed using assets from Freepik.com

This workbook
belongs to

_____

Table of Contetnts

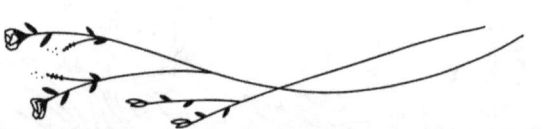

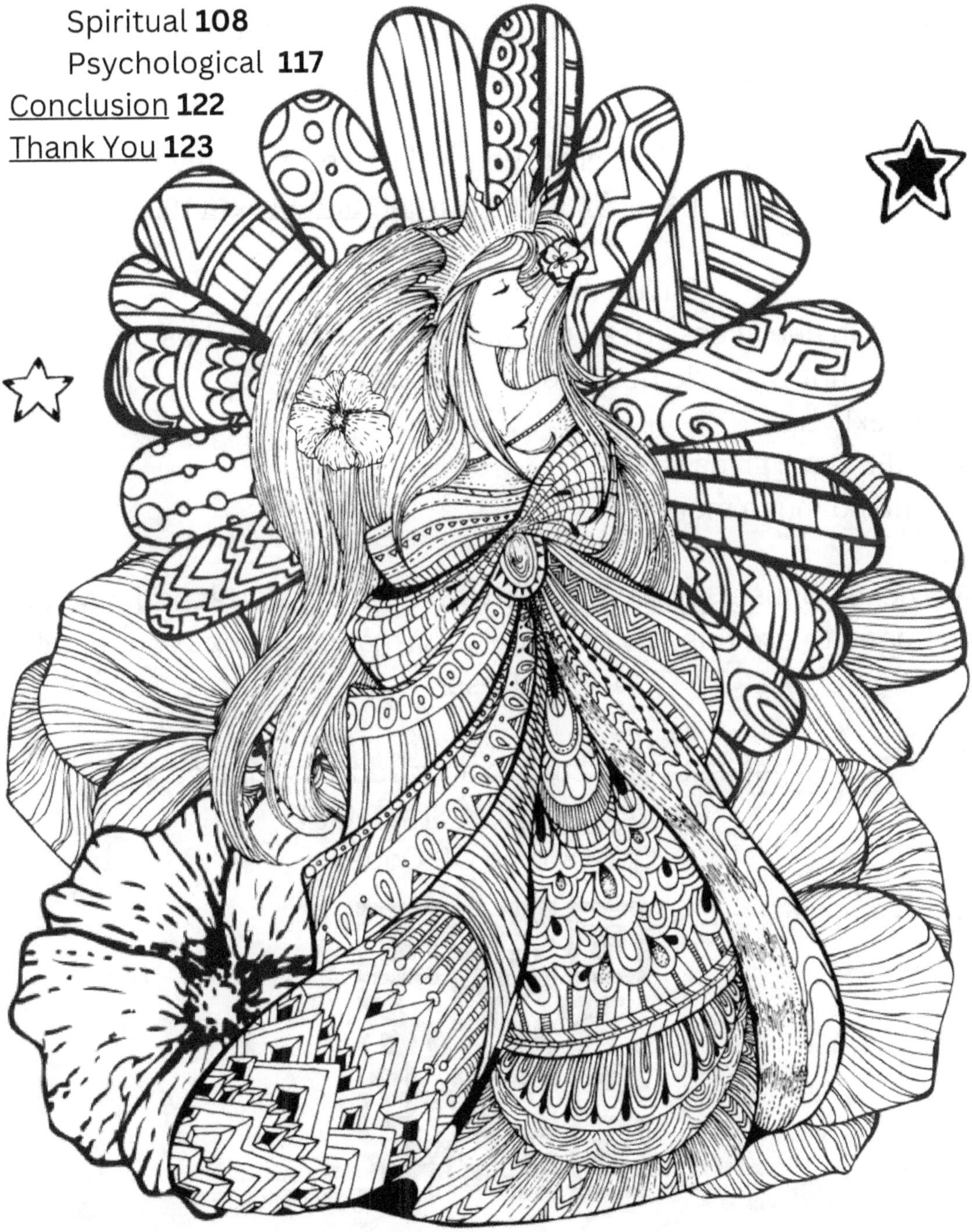

5 FREE Gifts!

Hey there! To help you along your journey. I've created 5 FREE Bonuses. You can get instant access by signing up to my email newsletter below:

On top of the 5 free gifts, you will be added to my new
<u>Platinum Level Reader Appreciation Program!</u>

You are entitled to all of this...
- First in line access to all my exclusive book launches
- Discount that I do not offer anywhere else
- Weekly tips
- FREE book giveaways
- And so much more

All these bonuses are 100% free with no strings attached. You do not need to provide any personal information except your email address:

To get instant access to all resources for free
GO TO: **OBIEZ.COM/SLWT-GIFT**
Or Scan the QR Code

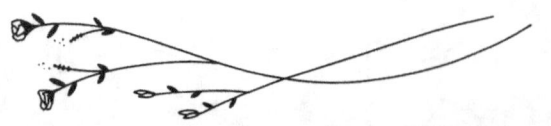

Mindfulness Journal for Teens

- 5 Minutes Daily Journaling to Reduce Anxiety and Live in the Present Moment
- Step by Step guidance and exercise to help teens cultivate mindfulness
- Encourage Teens to engage in self-reflection to foster a deeper understanding of themselves
- Cultivate appreciation and positivity
- Strategies and techniques for managing difficult emotions and building resilience

Mindfulness, Self-Love, and Meditation for Teens

- How to Insert Mindfulness, Self-love, and Meditation into your routine
- Eliminate Stress in Your Daily Routine
- Practical Guides for Mindfulness and Meditation
- How to Gain Self-Confidence and Conquer Your Dreams
- How to Stay Positive and Face Difficult Days

 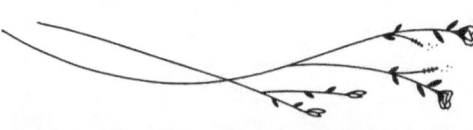

Anxiety Relief Guide

- How Anxiety Creeps Up and How to Avoid It
- 4 Practical Tools to Empower Yourself to Handle Your Emotions
- A Simple but Extremely Effective Technique to Treat Panic Attacks
- Little Known Secret to Be Socially Fearless
- And Much More...

The Power² Of Gratitude for Teens

- The Secret to Gratitude in Teens
- 5 Ways Gratitude Can Exponentiate a Teen's Life
- How a Simple Action Can Improve Your Family's Relationship
- And Much More...

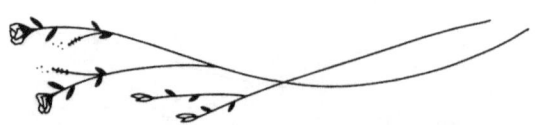

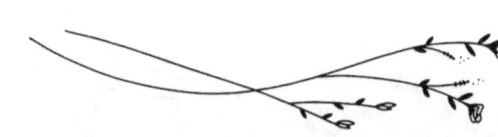

Guided Audio Meditation For Good Vibes

- 4 Audio Guided Meditations
- Quick Meditations to be used anywhere

To get instant access to all resources for free
GO TO: **OBIEZ.COM/SLWT-GIFT**
Or Scan the QR Code

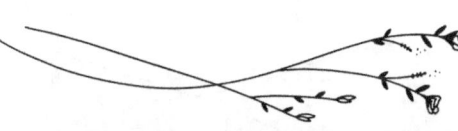

Hey Beautiful!

If I give you a plain paper and ask you to paint the perfect image of yourself that comes to your mind, what would the image look like?

I know different ideas would start popping into your head right now. However, I want you to know that regardless of the image you finally settle with, you holding the pencil is the only one responsible for what you draw, whether beautiful or ugly.

Now I want you to think of your life as a plain sheet of paper handed over to you – you decide the paper's fate by drawing a picture of who you are and what you want to become. The ink and pencil only influence the shade of the image drawn; they aren't in complete control – the person holding the pencil is. So if you want your image to be beautiful, which in this case is your life, you have to own it, be true to yourself, and love yourself! You have to be intentional about every stroke you draw. What you become lies in your hand!

I understand that in a world filled with imposter syndrome, self-doubt, and difficulty navigating challenging situations, loving yourself in its entirety is easier said than done, especially for teenagers.

I know this because, as a teenager, life was very stressful for me. I've tried to change things about myself – how I talk, how I walk, the kind of clothes I wear, the friends I move with, etc. I wanted to be like the other cool kids that looked perfect, or so I thought. I tried to fit in and not look different from others. I thought if others could accept and like me, I'd have good reasons to love myself.

 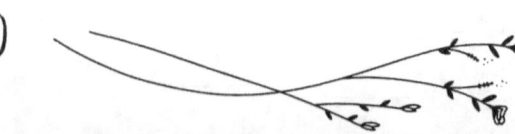

I was constantly worried about how I looked, my performance in school, societal pressures, and my relationships with others. It was so easy for me to lose focus, and every day, I felt like I was never good enough. I would look at myself in the mirror and tear myself apart with so many criticisms – there was nothing to love about me.

It got worse as I was called skinny, ugly, and body shamed by other kids in school. Life was terrible, and waking up to face my troubles every morning was scary. So, I can understand if you also have internal battles preventing you from living your best life.

Regardless of how bad you think your teenage years are, how you see your natural features or your family background, I can assure you that when you accept yourself just the way you are by practicing self-love, you will find life easier and less stressful. You'll become happier and feel more fulfilled. As a result, you will exude positive energy and do well in school, with people, and with your career.

But how do you practice self-love when there are so many things you don't like about yourself? I've repeatedly asked myself this same question but couldn't get any reasonable explanation. It was when I embarked on a journey to self-discovery that I could truly understand the concept of self-love.

Of course, you don't have to be perfect; no one is. But the truth is, everyone has flaws and having them doesn't make you any less human. I realized that accepting things that I can't change shows that I care about my life, and no form of negative talk can tear me down.

When I started practicing self-love, regardless of my flaws, I had the confidence to take on new challenges, cope with difficult situations, and always strive to do my best.

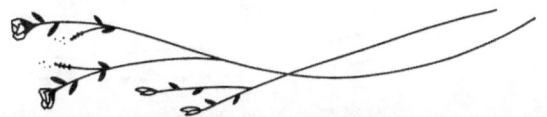 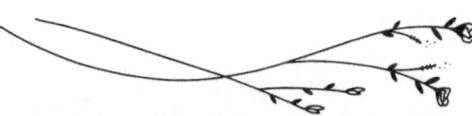

I know I make self-love sound easy, but I can't ignore the fact that it's pretty challenging. Thankfully, just like with any skill, self-love can be learned; when you do, it's life-transforming.

Self-love can change your life. When you flip the script on limiting beliefs, negative self-talk, and self-doubts, you are changing the course of your life. Yes, self-love is that powerful.

Seeing my experience and knowing many teen girls struggle with accepting and loving themselves inspired me to compile this workbook. This book is a collection of credible research and personal experience.

Use this book as your safe space to deal with peer pressure, overcome insecurities, and practice self-love. This book will provide you with tools to conquer your doubts and unlock a healthy mindset. You'll find research-backed, creative, and fun activities you can reflect on and have a better approach to life.

Think about your life. What do you think you could do differently if you had real self-confidence? What would you do when you genuinely believe in yourself? How would you and others feel about yourself when you truly love yourself?

Know that self-love isn't selfish. It is just a way to show that you are deserving of love. It's a way of treating yourself with respect, valuing your feelings, and embracing who you are.

When you deprive yourself of love, life will feel challenging. It will feel like you're fighting a battle you can't win. You deserve to enjoy life – you're worthy of love and many possibilities. Start the journey here.
Stay with me as you take the first step toward living a happier and more fulfilling life.

Chapter 1:
Understand The Concept Of Self-Love

Everyone's been talking about self-love, and it sure does sound amazing. But have you ever wondered what it means and why it's so important?

Before we can practice self-love, we need to understand what it means. It's not just about saying nice things to yourself in the mirror (although that can be fun too!).

This first chapter will discuss all you need to know about self-love. Now, let's get started!

What is Self-Love?

Imagine you have a friend and treat them with so much kindness, respect, and care. You always encourage them, celebrate their achievements, and support them through tough times. Well, guess what? That's what self-love is but in this case, directed toward yourself.

Self-love means deep appreciation and acceptance of yourself, flaws, and everything about you. It's about treating yourself like your own best friend and giving yourself the same love and attention you would give to someone you genuinely care about. It's not about being selfish or thinking you're better than others but about recognizing your worth and valuing yourself.

When you practice self-love, you prioritize your own well-being and happiness. You make choices that are good for you, both physically and mentally. You are permitting yourself to say no when something doesn't feel right or taking breaks when needed. It's about setting healthy boundaries and not letting others take advantage of you.

Self-love also means embracing your strengths, talents, and unique qualities. Instead of comparing yourself to others and feeling bad about yourself, you celebrate your accomplishments and focus on your growth. You appreciate your beauty, both inside and out, and recognize that you are enough just as you are.

Self-love isn't something that happens overnight. It's a lifelong journey of learning to be kind to yourself and nurturing a positive relationship with yourself. It involves practicing self-care, which can bring you joy and make you feel good, whether taking a bubble bath, spending time with loved ones, reading a book, or pursuing a hobby you love.

When you genuinely love yourself, it has a ripple effect on your life. You attract healthier relationships, make better choices, and feel more confident pursuing your dreams. You become resilient and better equipped to handle challenges that come your way.

Why You Might Be Lacking Self-Love

One reason you might be lacking self-love is because you're comparing yourself to others. It's easy to look at people around you, whether friends, celebrities, or influencers on social media, and feel like you don't measure up. But remember, everyone is unique and has their journey. Comparing yourself to others only leads to self-doubt and can make it hard to love yourself.

Another reason could be negative self-talk. That's when you have a habit of being hard on yourself and constantly criticizing or doubting your abilities.

Sometimes, the pressure to meet certain expectations from family, friends, or society can make it challenging to love yourself truly. You might feel like you must fit into a specific mold or be someone you're not just to be accepted or loved. But remember, you are unique and worthy of love just as you are. You don't need to be someone else. Embrace your individuality and surround yourself with people who appreciate you for who you truly are.

Another factor could be past experiences or traumas that have affected your self-esteem. Sometimes, negative experiences or hurtful comments from others can linger and make it hard to love yourself fully. It's essential to talk to someone you trust, like a counselor, a friend, or a family member, who can help you process those emotions and work toward healing.

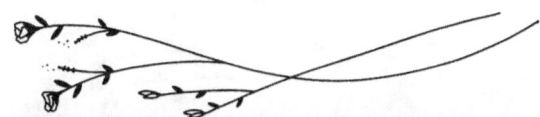 

Lastly, taking care of yourself physically, emotionally, and mentally plays a significant role in self-love. If you're neglecting your well-being or constantly putting others before yourself, it can leave you feeling drained and unloved. Ensure you prioritize self-care activities that bring you joy and help you recharge. This could include hobbies, exercise, spending time with loved ones, or practicing mindfulness and relaxation techniques

I am worthy of love, including my imperfections I grow with self-compassion

Benefits of Practicing Self-Love

Self-love has many tremendous benefits, especially for a teen girl like you. Let's take a look at some of them.

- **Boosts Confidence**

When you practice self-love, you start embracing your unique qualities and strengths. It helps you develop a positive self-image and boosts your confidence. You'll feel more comfortable in your own body and have the courage to take on new challenges.

- **Improves Mental Health**

Self-love plays a crucial role in your mental well-being. It helps you cultivate a positive mindset which improves your mental health. When you love yourself, you're more likely to have better self-esteem, cope with stress more effectively, and handle difficult emotions resiliently.

- **Nurtures Healthy Relationships**

When you love and accept yourself, you set healthy boundaries and surround yourself with people who genuinely care about you. Practicing self-love helps you recognize toxic relationships and avoid them. You'll attract positive and supportive friendships that uplift and inspire you.

- **Enhances Self-Care**

Self-love encourages you to prioritize your well-being. It means taking care of yourself physically, emotionally, and mentally. You'll learn to listen to your body's needs. Doing so gives you more energy to pursue your passions and goals.

- **Cultivates Resilience**

Life can be challenging, and setbacks are a part of the journey. Self-love equips you with the resilience to bounce back from failures and disappointments. When you love yourself, you believe in your abilities and learn from setbacks rather than letting them define you. This resilience helps you grow and thrive in the face of obstacles.

- Promotes Healthy Body Image

Society often bombards us with unrealistic beauty standards, negatively impacting our self-esteem. Self-love helps you embrace your body just the way it is. You'll focus on your health rather than your external appearance alone. You'll appreciate the uniqueness of your body and treat it with kindness through healthy habits and self-care.

- Inspires Personal Growth

When you practice self-love, you prioritize your personal growth and development. You'll set goals that align with your passions and values. When you believe in yourself and your abilities, you'll be motivated to step out of your comfort zone, learn new skills, and explore new opportunities. Self-love creates a foundation for continuous growth and self-improvement.

Obstacles to Self-love

Sometimes, some obstacles can make it challenging to love yourself truly. Let's talk about a few of these obstacles.

- Comparison

One big obstacle to self-love is comparing yourself to others. It's easy to look at someone else's achievements, appearance, or popularity and feel you need to improve. But remember, everyone is unique and has their journey. Instead of comparing yourself, focus on your strengths and accomplishments. Celebrate your own progress and be proud of who you are.

- Negative self-talk

We all have that little voice inside our heads that can be critical. Negative self-talk is when you constantly put yourself down, doubt your abilities, or believe you're not worthy of love and success. It's important to recognize this negative self-talk and challenge it. Replace those negative voices with positive affirmations and remind yourself of your worth and potential.

- Unrealistic expectations

Society often bombards us with unrealistic expectations of how we should look, act, or be. These expectations can create pressure and make it hard to love ourselves as we are. However, beauty comes in all shapes and sizes. So, embrace your individuality and focus on your happiness and well-being rather than trying to fit into someone else's mold.

- Past experiences

Past experiences, such as failures, rejections, or hurtful comments, can sometimes linger in our minds and affect our self-esteem. Remember, your past does not define you. Learn from those experiences, grow stronger, and use them as stepping stones to improve yourself. Don't let the past hold you back from loving and accepting who you are today.

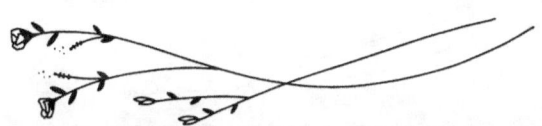 

- Lack of self-care

Caring for yourself mentally, physically, and emotionally is essential for self-love. If you neglect self-care, it becomes harder to appreciate and value yourself. Make time for activities that bring you joy, and practice self-care rituals like exercise, healthy eating, and getting enough rest. Be gentle to yourself with and prioritize your well-being.

Quiz To Check Your Self-Love Level

Before I share practical tips you can use to attain self-love, I'd like you to take a self-love quiz. This quiz will help you know your starting point –how much work you need to do on this self-love journey. Now, the following statements will help determine whether you actually love yourself a little, a lot, or not at all. For each statement give it a score from 1 to 10.

1. You know who you are, and you know what matters to you and what makes you happy.

Strongly Disagree | | | | | | | | | Strongly Agree
| 1 | 2 | 3 | 4 | 5 | 6 | 7 | 8 | 9 | 10 |

2. You are a good person and always do your best for yourself.

Strongly Disagree | | | | | | | | | Strongly Agree
| 1 | 2 | 3 | 4 | 5 | 6 | 7 | 8 | 9 | 10 |

3. You know what you want and are committed to achieving your dreams.

Strongly Disagree | | | | | | | | | Strongly Agree
| 1 | 2 | 3 | 4 | 5 | 6 | 7 | 8 | 9 | 10 |

4. You follow your inner guidance and do not allow others' opinions to stop you from pursuing what you want.

Strongly Disagree | | | | | | | | | Strongly Agree
| 1 | 2 | 3 | 4 | 5 | 6 | 7 | 8 | 9 | 10 |

5. You know you aren't perfect, and you're allowed to make mistakes because you're human.

Strongly Disagree | | | | | | | | | Strongly Agree
| 1 | 2 | 3 | 4 | 5 | 6 | 7 | 8 | 9 | 10 |

6. You cut yourself some slack and practice self-compassion when you fail instead of being self-critical.

Strongly Disagree | | | | | | | | | Strongly Agree
| 1 | 2 | 3 | 4 | 5 | 6 | 7 | 8 | 9 | 10 |

7. You take some time out for yourself when you feel stressed and overwhelmed.

Strongly Disagree | | | | | | | | | Strongly Agree
| 1 | 2 | 3 | 4 | 5 | 6 | 7 | 8 | 9 | 10 |

8. You transform or end a relationship when it's unhealthy because you value your peace of mind.

Strongly Disagree   Strongly Agree

| 1 | 2 | 3 | 4 | 5 | 6 | 7 | 8 | 9 | 10 |

9. Your happiness isn't dependent on your relationships – you feel good about yourself regardless of your relationships with others.

Strongly Disagree   Strongly Agree

| 1 | 2 | 3 | 4 | 5 | 6 | 7 | 8 | 9 | 10 |

10. You feel grateful for what you have; even if you aren't where you want to be yet, you'll get there.

Strongly Disagree   Strongly Agree

| 1 | 2 | 3 | 4 | 5 | 6 | 7 | 8 | 9 | 10 |

11. You prioritize rest, sleep, physical health, and exercise.

Strongly Disagree   Strongly Agree

| 1 | 2 | 3 | 4 | 5 | 6 | 7 | 8 | 9 | 10 |

12. You don't compare yourself to others because no good ever comes from such.

Strongly Disagree   Strongly Agree

| 1 | 2 | 3 | 4 | 5 | 6 | 7 | 8 | 9 | 10 |

13. You love your body as it is because everyone is beautiful in their own way.

Strongly Disagree   Strongly Agree

| 1 | 2 | 3 | 4 | 5 | 6 | 7 | 8 | 9 | 10 |

14. You know you're beautiful and would look into the mirror to only tell yourself positive things.

Strongly Disagree   Strongly Agree

| 1 | 2 | 3 | 4 | 5 | 6 | 7 | 8 | 9 | 10 |

15. You have a healthy balance of work and play; even when you have a lot going on, you will find time for something fun daily.

Strongly Disagree   Strongly Agree

| 1 | 2 | 3 | 4 | 5 | 6 | 7 | 8 | 9 | 10 |

Hey there, amazing soul! You've aced the self-love quiz like a pro, and now it's time to unveil your self-love prowess. Total up your scores from each question to find out where you stand on your self-love journey.

- 14 to 60 points: Embrace the Growth

If your total points fall within this range, no worries at all! You're at a phase where self-love is just starting to bloom, and that's totally fine. It's the perfect opportunity to sow the seeds of self-compassion and watch them grow into a beautiful garden of self-acceptance. This workbook is your supportive companion, offering practical tips, exercises, and uplifting stories to help you nurture that self-love. From building confidence to self-care practices and overcoming self-doubt, we'll walk this path together. Embrace the journey, and let's cultivate that self-love!

- 61 to 100 points: You're the Self-Love Pro

In this range, you've showcased some serious self-love skills, and we're all cheering for you! You've already got a knack for embracing your worth and showering yourself with love. But you know what? There's always room to grow even stronger. This workbook is your secret weapon to elevate your self-love game further. Dive into its pages to discover advanced self-care techniques, learn how to set healthy boundaries, and delve into the world of positive affirmations and gratitude. Let's take your self-love to the next level and continue to thrive together!

- 101 to 150 points: Bow Down, You're the Self-Love Queen

Whoa, bow down, everyone! You've reached the pinnacle of self-love royalty. Your high total points prove that you know how to rule your self-love kingdom with grace and confidence. Your self-acceptance is rock solid, and you inspire others with your self-assuredness. Even at this level, this workbook can still be your trusted companion. Dive into its pages to find strategies to maintain and spread your self-love magic.

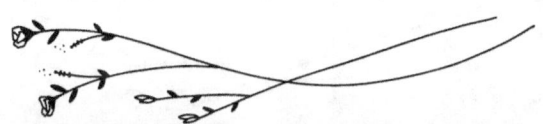 

Explore mindfulness practices, journaling exercises for self-reflection, and ways to inspire and support others in their self-love journey. Let's continue to flourish as the incredible self-love queen you are!

No matter where your score lands, remember that self-love is a continuous journey of growth and learning. Embrace every step, and don't be afraid to seek support and resources to boost your self-love game. This workbook is your go-to guide, providing you with tools and inspiration to love yourself fiercely, cherish your uniqueness, and rock on with that amazing spirit of yours! You're an unstoppable force, and the world is lucky to have someone as awesome as you!

Practical Tips for Self-Love

Self-love is super important, especially during the teenage years when things can get overwhelming. So, here are some practical tips for practicing self-love:

- Embrace your uniqueness

Remember, you're one-of-a-kind! Embrace your quirks, talents, and everything that makes you unique. Celebrate your individuality, and don't be afraid to be yourself.

- Positive self-talk

Pay attention to the way you talk to yourself. Replace negative thoughts with positive ones. Instead of saying, "I can't do it," try saying, "I can do anything I set my mind to." It might take some practice, but positive self-talk can make a huge difference in how you feel about yourself.

- Take care of your body

Your body is amazing and deserves to be taken care of. Fuel it with nutritious food, stay active, and get enough sleep. Remember to listen to your body and give it the rest it needs.

- Set boundaries

It's essential to set boundaries to protect your well-being. Learn to say no when you feel overwhelmed or when something doesn't align with your values. It's okay to prioritize yourself and your needs.

- Practice self-care

Find activities that make you feel good and relaxed. It could be anything from taking a bath, reading a book, listening to music, or walking in nature. Taking time for yourself and doing things you enjoy is a great way to show self-love.

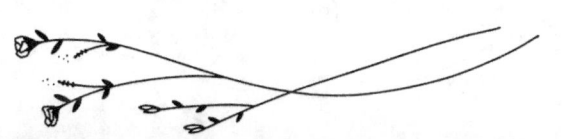 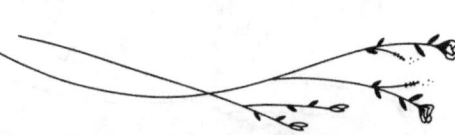

- Surround yourself with positive people

Surround yourself with people who lift you and support you. Spend time with friends who appreciate you for who you are and encourage your dreams and goals. Positive relationships can have a tremendous impact on your self-esteem.

- Celebrate your accomplishments

Take the time to acknowledge and celebrate your achievements, big or small. Whether acing a test, completing a project, or learning a new skill, give yourself a pat on the back. Recognizing your accomplishments boosts your self-confidence.

- Practice gratitude

Take a moment each day to reflect on what you're grateful for. Practicing gratitude redirects your attention to the positive elements of your life and cultivates a sense of contentment.

Activity 1:
Gratitude Journal

For this activity, you'll need to find a quiet and comfortable space.

- What are three things you appreciate about yourself? Write them down.
- Reflect on your qualities, strengths, or achievements that make you proud.
- Repeat this activity every day, adding new entries each time you do it.
- Take a moment to read your previous entries and embrace the positivity they bring.

QUALITTIES

STRENGTHS

ACHIEVEMENTS

Activity 2:
Positive Affirmations

For this activity, you'll need sticky notes and markers.
- Write down positive affirmations on sticky notes.
- Stick the notes in places you'll see them frequently, such as your mirror, study desk, or wardrobe.
- Every time you encounter a note, take a deep breath and say the affirmation aloud, embracing its truth.

Here are some examples:

I am Enough!

I deserve love and Respect

I am beautiful inside and outside

My uniqueness is my strengh

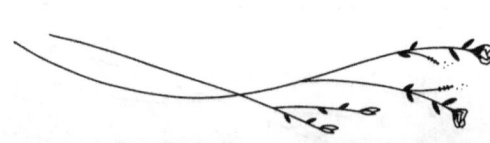

Now, let's write some of your own.

This page was intentionally left blank

Activity 3:
Mindful Self-Care

This is quite easy!

- Set aside a dedicated "me-time" each day, even if it's just 15 minutes.
- Find a quiet and peaceful place to relax.
- Participate in fun activities that bring you joy and relaxation, such as reading, drawing, or soothing baths.
- Embrace the present moment and allow yourself to be fully present with your thoughts and emotions.
- Write a list of activities you enjoy and tick the box as you complete them

Activities

☐ _____   ☐ _____

☐ _____   ☐ _____

☐ _____   ☐ _____

☐ _____   ☐ _____

☐ _____   ☐ _____

☐ _____   ☐ _____

☐ _____   ☐ _____

☐ _____   ☐ _____

☐ _____   ☐ _____

☐ _____   ☐ _____

☐ _____   ☐ _____

☐ _____   ☐ _____

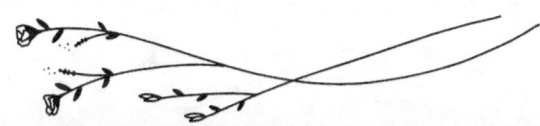 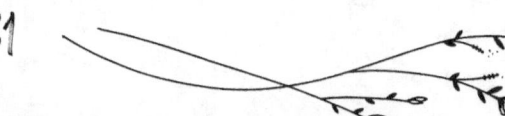

Activity 4:
Love Letter to Yourself

For this activity
- Sit in a comfortable and calm environment.
- Start writing a heartfelt love letter to yourself.
- Express gratitude for your unique qualities in the letter.
- Acknowledge your achievements and personal growth.
- Forgive yourself for any perceived flaws or mistakes.
- Highlight the reasons why you love and value yourself.
- Encourage and affirm yourself.

I LOVE ME

xoxo

Dear me

Activity 5:
Mirror Affirmations

For this activity, you'll need just a mirror.

- Stand in front of a mirror, looking into your own eyes.
- Take a deep breath and speak positive affirmations to yourself.

Examples can be:

1. I am beautiful just as I am.
2. I radiate confidence and self-love.
3. I am deserving of all the good things in life.
4. I embrace my imperfections as part of my unique beauty.

Affirmations

_____
_____
_____
_____
_____
_____
_____
_____
_____
_____
_____
_____
_____
_____
_____
_____
_____
_____
_____
_____
_____
_____
_____
_____
_____
_____
_____
_____
_____
_____
_____

 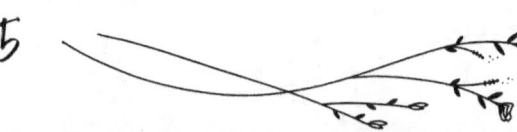

Activity 6:
Acts of Self-Kindness

This entails listing kind gestures or activities that make you feel loved and appreciated. Examples can be :

- Take a walk in nature.
- Treat yourself to a favorite meal.
- Practice a hobby you enjoy.
- Write in your journal.
- Have a pampering self-care session.
- Commit to performing one act of self-kindness every day for a week.

Reflect on how these actions make you feel and impact your self-love journey.

And that's it for this chapter! Stay with me as we'll discuss self-awareness in the next chapter.

Activity _____

How it made you feel? _____

_____

_____

Activity _____

How it made you feel? _____

_____

_____

Activity _____

How it made you feel? _____

_____

_____

 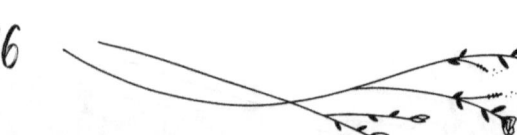

Chapter 2:
Become More Self-Aware

As a teenager, life can be pretty hectic with school, extracurricular activities, chores at home, part-time jobs, college preparations, family obligations, and even a social life to juggle with. With all these, self-awareness might be the last thing on your mind. But trust me; self-awareness can help you more than you realize.

Self-awareness entails taking a closer look at who you are - your values, beliefs, role models, goals, challenges, and even your shortcomings. Being self-aware means you become more intentional and purposeful instead of reacting to whatever is happening around you. It's like having a superpower that allows you to control your thoughts and emotions, even when faced with adversities. You become more true to yourself and can shine a positive light on those around you.

This chapter will discuss self-awareness and how you can become more self-aware.

What is Self-Awareness, and How Does It Help Teens?

Self-awareness means being aware of yourself, your thoughts, feelings, and behavior. It's like having a little voice inside you that helps you understand who you are, what you like, and why you do what you do.

Think of it this way: you have your unique personality, preferences, and motivations. Self-awareness is like having a personal expert who knows all about you. This expert helps you discover who you truly are and what makes you happy. It's like having a window into your mind.

For example, let's say you notice that you feel anxious before giving a presentation at school. Self-awareness helps you recognize this feeling and understand why it's happening. You may realize you're afraid of making mistakes or being judged by others. When you're self-aware, you can acknowledge these thoughts and emotions and find ways to cope.

So, think of self-awareness as having a friendly guide inside you, someone who knows you better than anyone else. A personal compass that helps you navigate life, understand yourself deeply, and make choices that align with your true identity.

Now, why is self-awareness crucial for teens? Well, first off, it helps you understand your emotions better. Sometimes, being a teenager can be a rollercoaster of emotions, right? You might feel happy one moment, sad the next, and angry after that. When you're self-aware, you can recognize and name these emotions, which can be super helpful in figuring out how to deal with them.

Self-awareness also helps you pinpoint your strengths and weaknesses. Everyone has different talents and abilities, and being aware of what you're good at and what you might struggle with can help you make better decisions. It can guide you in choosing hobbies or future career paths that align with your strengths and passions.

Another cool thing about self-awareness is that it helps you improve your relationships with others. When you're aware of your thoughts and feelings, it's easier to understand and empathize with others. You can also recognize when you might react in certain ways because of your insecurities or biases, which can help you be more open-minded and accepting of others.

 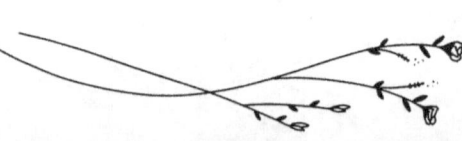

Self-awareness also gives you the power to take control of your life. It helps you set goals and make choices that align with your values and what you truly want. Instead of just going along with what others expect from you, you become the captain of your ship, steering it in the direction that feels right for you.

When you're self-aware, you can make choices that reflect who you are and what you want. You're not just going along with the crowd or doing things because it's what's expected of you. Instead, you can shape your path and create a life that resonates with your deepest desires.

Improving Your Self-Awareness

So, how can you improve your self-awareness? Well, it's not a day's job; it takes time and practice.

Pay attention to your thoughts.
Have you ever stopped to pay attention to the thoughts that float around in your mind? Those little ideas and patterns that seem to pop up out of nowhere? These thoughts play a more prominent role in your life than you might realize.

Take a moment to reflect on the nature of your thoughts. Are they generally positive or negative? Do they make you feel good or bring you down? The quality of our thoughts can significantly impact our overall well-being and success.

Here's the exciting part: you can choose which thoughts to hold onto and which to let go of. When you're aware of your thoughts, you can consciously decide which ones serve you well and which hinder your progress.

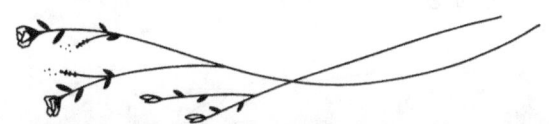 

Let's say you notice a negative thought creeping into your mind, telling you you're not good enough or you'll never achieve your goals. Instead of letting that thought drag you down, you can actively replace it with a more positive and empowering thought. You can remind yourself of your strengths, achievements, and potential to overcome challenges.

It's like being the director of your mental movie. You can rewrite the script and create a more uplifting and encouraging storyline.

- **Tune into your emotions.**

Emotions can be like a roller coaster, and it's important to recognize and understand them. Take a moment to check in with yourself and ask, "How am I feeling right now?" Maybe you're happy, sad, excited, or stressed.

Acknowledging your emotions helps you understand why you feel a certain way and find healthy ways to cope with them.

- **Observe your actions and behaviors.**

Notice how you behave in different situations. Are you confident in social settings, or do you tend to shy away? Are you an active listener, or do you interrupt others? Paying attention to your actions can help you identify areas where you want to improve or change.

- **Reflect.**

Take some time to think about your strengths, weaknesses, and values. What are you good at? What challenges you? What's important to you in life? Understanding your strengths can boost your confidence, and your weaknesses can guide your growth.

- **Seek feedback from others.**

Sometimes, we may not fully see ourselves as others do. Ask your trusted friends, family members, or mentors for honest opinions. They can provide valuable insights that you might not have considered before.

Improving your self-awareness is an ongoing process. It's like peeling layers of an onion to discover more about yourself. The more you understand yourself, the better equipped you'll be to make choices that align with who you truly are.

Activity 1:
Self-Reflection Exercise

This activity will help you explore and improve your self-awareness. Take your time and reflect on each question and prompt. Feel free to write down your thoughts, ideas, and experiences. Remember, there are no right or wrong answers. Ensure you enjoy the process of self-discovery!

Take a moment to think about your identity, values, and beliefs. Now answer the following questions:

Who are you? Describe yourself in a few words.

_____
_____
_____
_____
_____
_____

What are some of your core values?

_____
_____
_____
_____
_____
_____

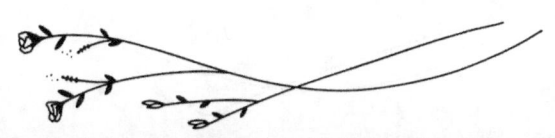 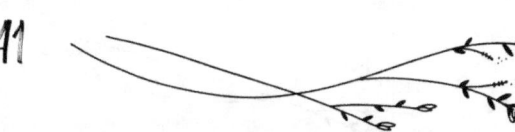

Why are they important to you?

_____
_____
_____
_____
_____
_____
_____

What are your passions and interests?

_____
_____
_____
_____
_____
_____
_____

How do they contribute to your sense of self?

_____
_____
_____
_____
_____
_____
_____

Activity 2:
Identifying Strengths and Weaknesses Exercise

Gaining insight into your strengths and weaknesses is essential for self-awareness.

- List three of your strengths and explain how they positively impact your life

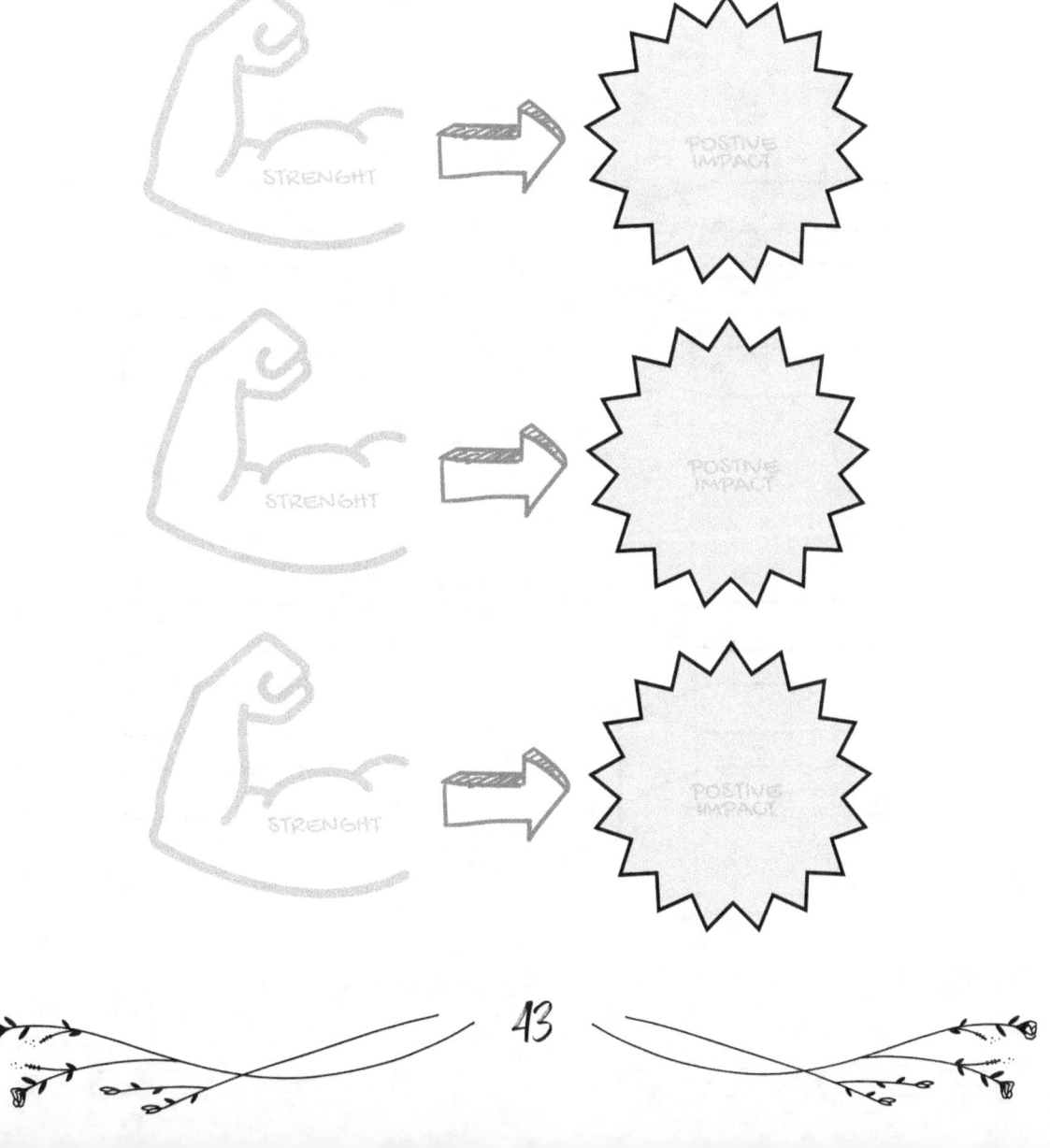

Identify three areas where you want to improve and turn them into actionable goals.

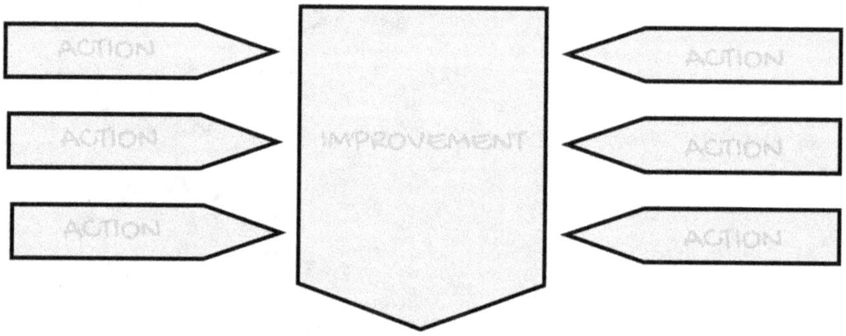

ACTION   ACTION

ACTION   IMPROVEMENT   ACTION

ACTION   ACTION

ACTION   ACTION

ACTION   IMPROVEMENT   ACTION

ACTION   ACTION

ACTION   ACTION

ACTION   IMPROVEMENT   ACTION

ACTION   ACTION

 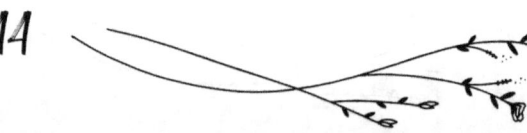

How do you handle criticism? Reflect on how you can use constructive feedback to grow and learn.

Write down inside the vase what you learned from feedbacks.

Activity 3:
Emotional Intelligence Exercise

Emotional intelligence means grasping and controlling your feelings, as well as recognizing and empathizing with others' emotions. Answer the following questions:

How do you typically express your emotions? Are there any emotions you struggle to express?

_____

_____

_____

_____

_____

Think of a recent situation when you handled your emotions effectively. Describe what happened and how you felt afterward.

_____

_____

_____

_____

_____

What strategies do you use to manage stress and maintain emotional balance?

_____

_____

_____

_____

_____

Activity 4:
Self-Care and Well-being Exercise

Taking care of yourself is essential for self-awareness. Respond to the following prompts:

How do you prioritize self-care in your daily life? Provide examples of activities or habits that make you feel rejuvenated.

_____
_____
_____
_____
_____

Reflect on your physical health. Are there any changes or improvements you would like to make?

_____
_____
_____
_____
_____

How does your mental and emotional well-being impact your overall self-awareness?

_____
_____
_____
_____
_____

Activity 5:
Relationships and Boundaries Exercise

Hey, fabulous! Buckle up for to dive into the world of boundaries and discover how you can rock 'em like a superstar while staying true to your fabulous self. So, grab your favorite funky pen and let's get this party started!

What's the Buzz About Boundaries?

Hold up, do you know what boundaries are? Think of them as your very own superhero shield, keeping your relationships healthy and protecting your happiness. Boundaries are like the lines you draw to show what's cool and what's not, all while making sure you feel safe and respected.

Let's break it down into some super cool boundary types:

- Physical Boundaries:

It's all about personal space, chica! It's about setting limits on hugs, personal stuff, and how close people get to you.

- Emotional Boundaries:

Emotions on lockdown! These boundaries help you decide how much you want to share and when you need some "me" time to deal with your feelings.

Time Boundaries: Time is precious, and it's up to you to decide how to spend it. Time boundaries help you manage how much time you give to others and how much you keep for yourself.

- Digital Boundaries:

Say hello to the digital realm! Digital boundaries involve taking charge of your online world, managing your privacy, and keeping a healthy balance with social media and screens.

 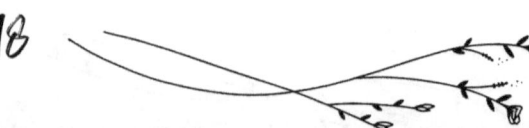

Now that you've got the scoop on boundaries, let's jam on how to let others know what's up:

1. Get Your Groove on and Know Yourself
Before you start dishing out boundaries like a pro, take a moment to tune into your needs, values, and what makes you feel comfortable. Knowing yourself is the first step to setting those super cool boundaries!

2. Unleash Your Inner Superstar and Be Clear
When you're ready to let others in on your boundaries, make sure to be crystal clear. Use your superstar confidence and rock those "I" statements to express how you feel and what you need. For example, instead of saying, "You're always all up in my business," you can say, "Hey, I feel more chill when we give each other some space."

3. Tune in and Rock Active Listening
Remember, communication is all about the give and take. It's time to bust out those rad active listening skills! Show that you're all ears, give some love, and keep an open mind. This sets the stage for a groovy conversation.

4. Flex Your Superpowers and Set Consequences
Sometimes, people may accidentally step over your boundaries. No biggie! Just let them know what's up and what might go down if they keep it up. You can say, "If you keep invading my personal space, I might have to go chill by myself for a bit."

5. Squad Goals: Seek Support
If you're feeling a bit unsure or if someone keeps crossing your boundaries, reach out to your trusted squad. Talk to a cool adult, a counselor, or a friend who can offer their rad advice and support. Teamwork makes the dream work!

 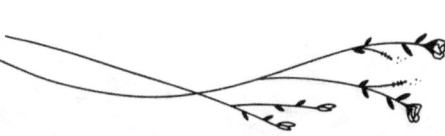

It's Your Time to Shine!

Remember, setting boundaries is like being a superhero of self-love. It shows that you've got mad respect for yourself and your well-being. So, go out there, let your boundaries shine, and build rockin' relationships based on respect and understanding. You've got the power, babe!

Now, let's grab those funky pens, doodle some boundary bling, and jot down Answering the following questions:

Reflect on a time when you felt your boundaries were crossed. How did you handle the situation, and what did you learn from it?

_____
_____
_____
_____
_____
_____

How do your relationships influence your self-awareness? Describe the impact of both positive and negative relationships.

_____
_____
_____
_____
_____

Take a moment to review your answers and reflect on the insights you gained through this activity. Remember that self-awareness is an ongoing journey, and it's okay to revisit and reassess your thoughts and feelings as you grow.

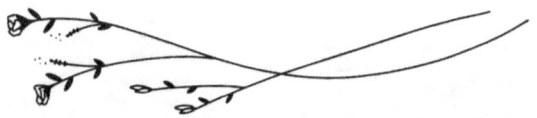 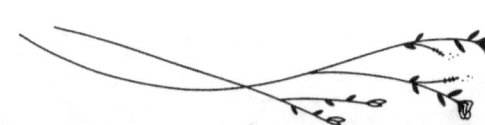

How To Deal With Difficult Emotions

Dealing with difficult emotions can be challenging, but remember, you're not alone. It's completely normal to experience a wide range of emotions as a teenager. So, let's dive into some tips to help you handle those challenging feelings.

- Recognize and accept your emotions.

The first step is acknowledging what you're feeling. It could be sadness, anger, frustration, or anything else. Feeling these emotions is okay; they're a natural part of being human. Embrace them rather than push them away.

- Permit yourself to feel.

Sometimes, we try to hide or suppress our emotions because we think they're wrong or weak. But guess what? It's perfectly okay to feel sad, angry, or upset. Allow yourself to experience those emotions fully without judgment.

- Find healthy ways to express yourself.

Bottling up emotions isn't healthy in the long run. Instead, try positively expressing yourself. You can write in a journal or engage in creative activities like drawing, painting, or playing an instrument. Find what works best for you.

- Take care of yourself physically.

Our emotional well-being is closely linked to our physical well-being. Engage in activities that make you feel good, like exercising, walking in nature, or practicing mindfulness and meditation. These can help reduce stress and bring a sense of calm.

- Seek support

Feel free to reach out for support when you need it. Talk to someone you trust. It could be a family member, close friend, counselor, or therapist. They can guide, lend a listening ear, and help you navigate difficult emotions.

- Practice self-compassion

Be kind to yourself. Understand that everyone goes through ups and downs, and making mistakes or feeling overwhelmed is okay. Treat yourself with the same compassion you'd offer a close friend.

- Develop healthy coping mechanisms.

Instead of resorting to negative coping mechanisms like unhealthy eating habits, substance abuse, or isolating yourself, try to develop healthier alternatives. Engage in activities like listening to music, reading, or your hobbies. These can help distract and uplift your mood.

Emotional Regulation Skills and Exercises

Dealing with difficult emotions can be challenging, but remember, you're not alone. It's completely normal to experience a wide range of emotions as a teenager. So, let's dive into some tips to help you handle those challenging feelings.

- Deep breathing

Breathing deeply can help you calm down when feeling stressed or overwhelmed. Breathe slowly through your nose, hold it for a few seconds, and breathe out through your mouth. Repeat this a few times, and you'll feel more relaxed.

- Positive self-talk

The way we talk to ourselves can impact our emotions. Instead of being hard on yourself, try using kind and encouraging words. For example, if you feel nervous about a test, remind yourself that you've studied and can do your best.

- Problem-solving

Sometimes our emotions arise from a specific problem or situation. In these cases, it can be helpful to break the problem down into smaller steps and develop solutions. This helps you feel more in control and less overwhelmed.

- Physical activity

Physical activities like dancing, running, or walking can help release tension and improve your mood. Also, it can distract you from negative thoughts.

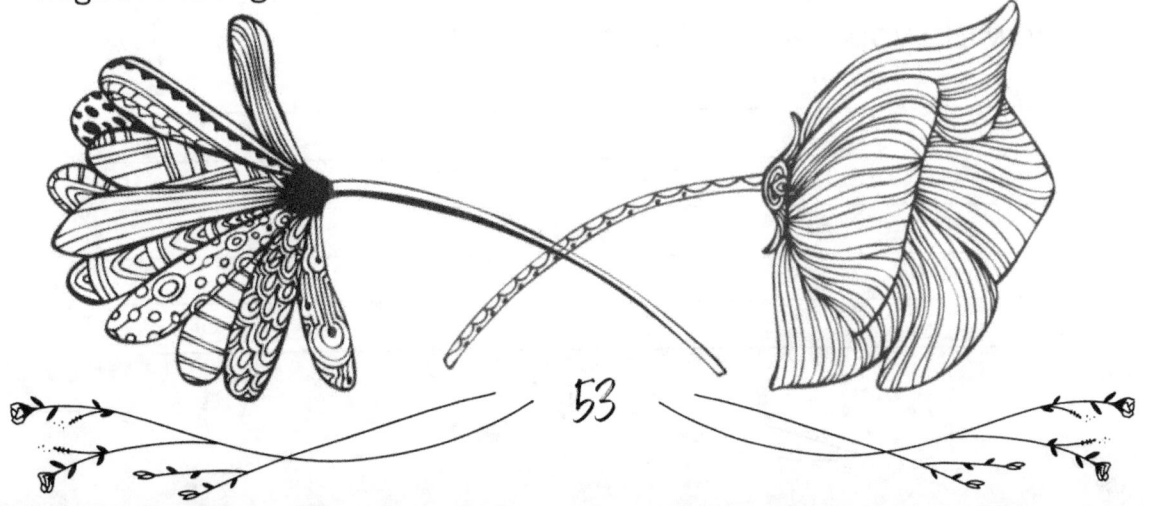

Activity 6:
Recognizing Your Emotions Exercise

Reflect on your emotions and use the following activity to help you better understand and manage difficult emotions.

Which three difficult emotions do you often experience?

_____
_____
_____
_____
_____
_____

Please choose one of the emotions and describe a recent situation that triggered it.

_____
_____
_____
_____
_____
_____

How did you react to this emotion?

_____
_____
_____
_____
_____
_____
_____

Activity 7:
Mindful Breathing

1 Find a quiet and comfortable place to sit. Close your eyes and take a deep breath through your nose, counting to four.

2 Hold your breath for a count of four.

3 Exhale slowly through your mouth, counting to five.

4 Repeat this cycle of breaths five times. Pay attention to how you feel before and after this exercise.

Activity 8:
Positive Affirmations

Mention three positive affirmations that resonate with you.

For example: "I am strong," "I am deserving of love and happiness," and "I have the power to overcome challenges."

Repeat these affirmations to yourself every morning for the next week. Notice how they make you feel and how they may impact your outlook.

Affirmation #1

Affirmation #2

Affirmation #3

I'm the captain of my thoughts, sailing through positivity!

Chapter 3:
Tweak Your Thought Patterns

Sometimes it feels like a constant stream of negative thoughts and self-criticism is swirling around in your head. It feels like your own thoughts are working against you. But don't worry; you're not alone. It's common for teens to go through this.

During adolescence, you're going through many changes and figuring out who you are. You want to feel good about yourself, be independent, and connect with others outside your family. It's all part of growing up. But along the way, you might face obstacles and start doubting yourself. It's completely normal.

If these negative thoughts and patterns keep repeating over time, they can start to take a toll on your mental health. They can make you feel angry and hopeless and even contribute to anxiety and depression. That's why it's essential to make some adjustments in how you think.

It's not about ignoring your challenges or pretending everything is perfect. It's about finding a balance and being kinder to yourself. It's all about training your mind to think differently. Instead of focusing on the negative aspects of yourself or your life, try to find the positives.

By doing so, you can support your mental well-being. It's like rewiring your brain to break the habit of negativity and start seeing the world, and yourself, in a more positive light.

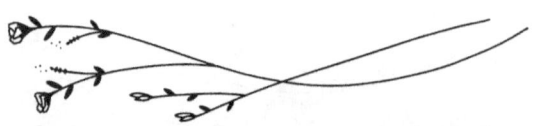 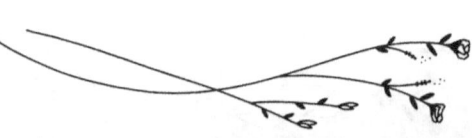

You're still growing and learning, and it's okay to have ups and downs. Just know you can change your thoughts and cultivate a more positive mindset.

What Are Self-Limiting Thoughts, And Why Do You Have Them?

Self-limiting thoughts are the little ideas or beliefs about ourselves that keep us from reaching our full potential. They often pop up in our minds and tell us what we can't do or are not good at. It's like having a tiny voice that's always doubting you. It might sound like this: "You're not smart enough," "You'll never be as good as others," or "What if you mess up and everyone laughs?" These thoughts come from a place of fear and insecurity, and they can hold us back if we let them.

We all have self-limiting thoughts occasionally, which can be a real bummer. They stop us from trying new things, taking risks, or believing in ourselves. They put a big cloud of doubt over our abilities and keep us in our comfort zones.

But here's the thing, self-limiting thoughts are not facts. They're just thoughts, and thoughts can be changed. You might be wondering, "Why do I have these thoughts in the first place?" Our minds are powerful, but sometimes they get too good at protecting us from potential failure or embarrassment. They try to keep us safe by telling us why we can't do something.

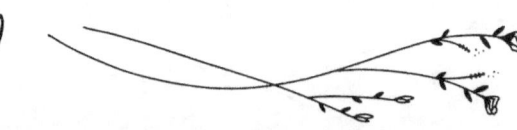

Self-limiting thoughts usually stem from our fears and insecurities. Sometimes, we're afraid of failing or making mistakes, so our mind tries to protect us by saying, "You can't do it, so don't even try." It's like a defense mechanism that wants to keep us safe in our comfort zones. And guess what? Our comfort zones can be boring and predictable. They might feel safe, but they also prevent us from experiencing new things and growing as individuals.

How To Tweak Your Thought Patterns And Think Positively

You must learn to tweak your thought patterns and think positively because your thoughts can significantly impact how you feel and navigate life. So, let's dive in and discover some helpful ways to make that happen!

- Be Aware of Your Thoughts

The first step is to pay attention to your thoughts. First off, take a moment to notice the patterns in your thoughts. Do you tend to think more negatively or positively? This is important because our thoughts can shape our overall outlook on life. If you often have negative thoughts, it's good to be aware of that and work on shifting them in a more positive direction.

Remember, you are the boss of your thoughts. You have the power to control them and decide what kind of thoughts you want to have. It might take some practice, but knowing your thoughts is the first step. Once you start paying attention, you'll be amazed at how much influence you have over them.

- Challenge Negative Thoughts

Sometimes, negative thoughts can sneak into our minds without us even noticing. They can make us feel down and unmotivated or even doubt ourselves. But guess what? We have the power to challenge those negative thoughts and turn things around!

The first step is to recognize when negative thoughts pop up. It could be something like, "I'm not good enough," "I'll never succeed," or "Nobody likes me." When you catch yourself thinking negatively, take a moment to pause and reflect. Ask yourself, "Are these thoughts true?"

You see, negative thoughts often exaggerate or twist reality. They tend to focus on the bad stuff while ignoring the good things about themselves or the situation. So, it's essential to challenge those negative thoughts and question their validity.

Start by examining the evidence. Is there any proof that supports these negative thoughts? Usually, you'll find that there is little evidence to back them up. It's like your mind is playing tricks on you! Remember that these thoughts are not entirely true or accurate reflections of who you are.

Next, try to find alternative, more positive perspectives. Ask yourself, "What other ways to look at this situation?" Consider the positive aspects of the things you've accomplished in the past. Maybe you had a setback, but that doesn't define your entire journey. There are always different angles to approach any situation.

Here comes the exciting part: replacing those negative thoughts with uplifting ones! Once you've challenged the negative thoughts, it's time to swap them out with positive ones. It could be something like, "I have unique talents and qualities," "I am capable of achieving my goals," or "I am surrounded by people who care about me."

When you consciously choose positive thoughts and repeat them to yourself, you're rewiring your brain to focus on the good stuff. It might take some time and practice, but trust me; it's worth it!

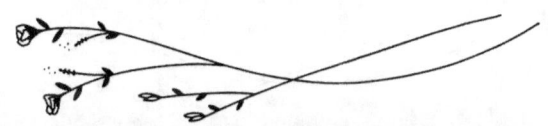 

- Practice Gratitude

Gratitude is an excellent tool for shifting your mindset toward positivity. Here's a simple exercise you can try every day. Take a moment to think about three things you're grateful for. They can be anything, from the big stuff to the little things that make you smile. It could be a sunny day that lifts your spirits or a compliment from a friend that makes you feel awesome.

Focusing on these positive things will train your mind to see more good stuff around you. It's like putting on a special pair of glasses that help you notice all the amazing things happening in your life. And guess what? The more you practice gratitude, the more you'll feel happier and more positive overall.

- Surround Yourself with Positivity

The people and things around you can greatly influence your thought patterns. Imagine being in a room filled with always happy, encouraging, and supportive people. How do you think you would feel? It's pretty great. That's the power of surrounding yourself with positivity.

First, choosing friends who bring out the best in you is crucial. Look for positive and supportive people who always have your back and make you feel good about yourself. Spending time with these friends will boost your mood and make you happier.

But it's not just about the people around you. The things you do and expose yourself to also play a significant role in your mindset. Engage in activities that make you happy and inspire you. Whether playing a sport, painting, dancing, or writing, pursue what brings you joy. These activities will lift your spirits and help you stay positive.

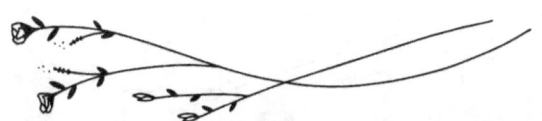 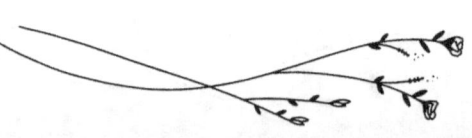

Consider what you consume, like books, movies, and podcasts. Have you ever noticed how certain stories or messages can make you feel motivated, inspired, or just plain good? Well, that's the power of positive influences. Seek books, movies, or podcasts promoting positivity, self-love, and personal growth. These can give you a fresh perspective on life, boost your confidence, and help you see the bright side.

Surrounding yourself with positivity isn't about ignoring negative experiences or pretending everything is perfect. It's about consciously focusing on the good things in life and surrounding yourself with people and influences that lift you, support you, and inspire you to be the best version of yourself.

- Practice Self-Compassion

It's crucial to be kind to yourself. You know how you're always there for your friend, cheering them up and supporting them when they feel down? Well, it's time to do the same for yourself!

First off, it's crucial to acknowledge your strengths and accomplishments. Give yourself a high-five when you do something well or achieve a goal. You could have aced a test, made a new friend, or learned a new skill. These are all reasons to celebrate and feel proud of yourself.

Life isn't always rainbows and sunshine. We all mess up sometimes, and that's okay! Instead of being too hard on yourself when things don't go as planned, try to be understanding and forgiving. Remember, making mistakes is part of being human. It's how we learn and grow. So be your cheerleader, your supporter, and your own best friend.

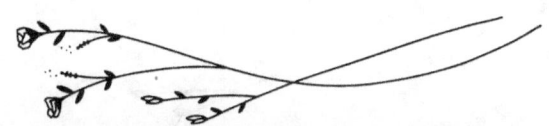 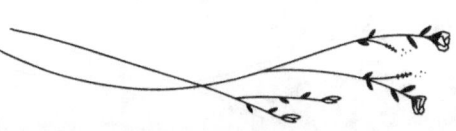

Activity 1:
Understanding Negative Thoughts

The objective is to identify and become aware of negative thoughts.

- Write three negative thoughts that frequently come to your mind.
- Reflect on why these thoughts might be harmful or limiting.
- What are positive thoughts that could replace each negative thought?
- Keep this list with you to refer to when negative thoughts arise.

Example:

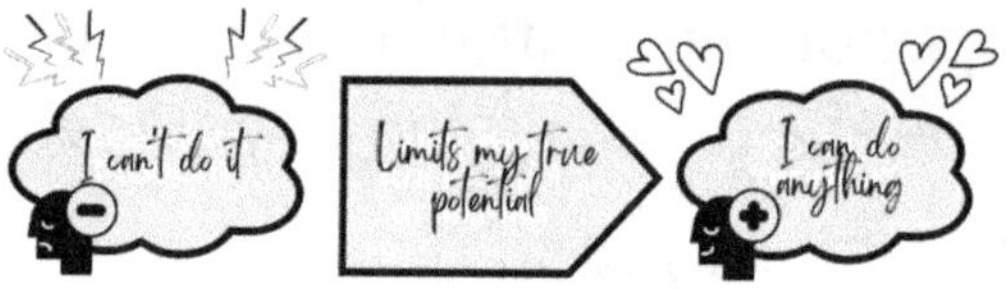

I can't do it → Limits my true potential → I can do anything

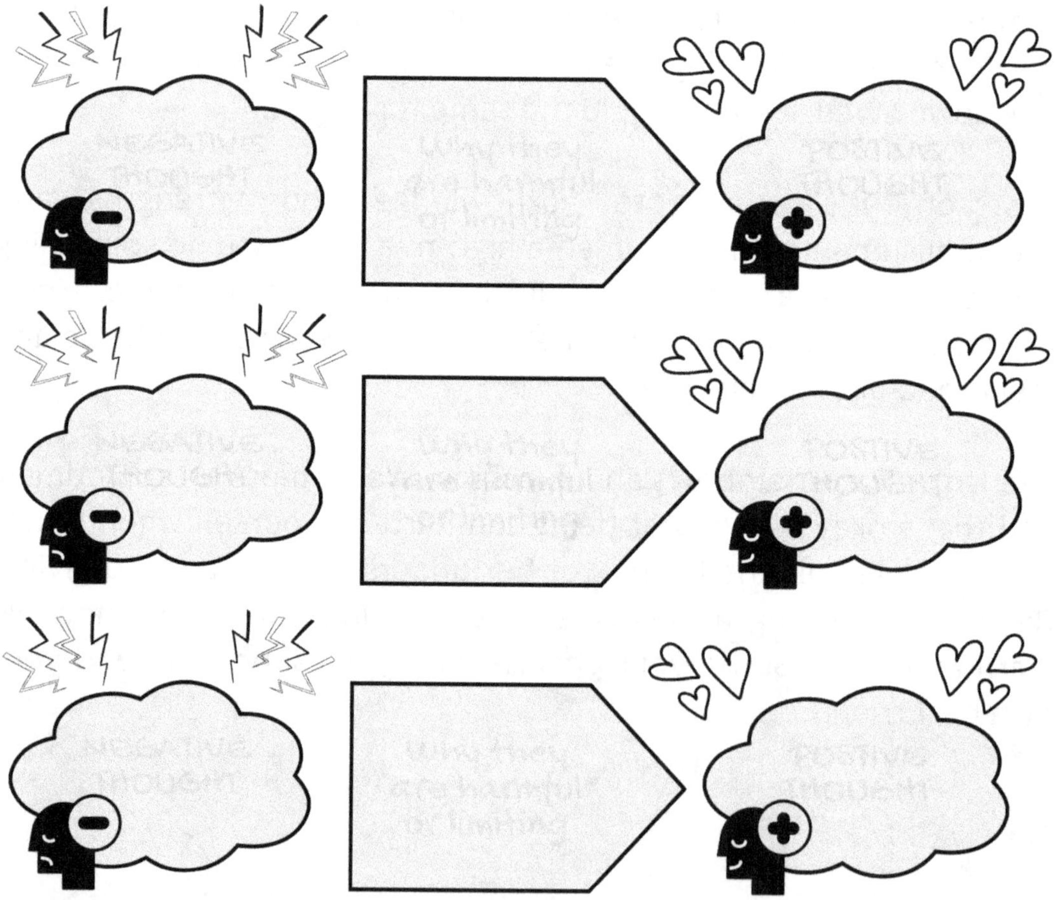

Activity 2:
Practicing Gratitude

The objective is to cultivate an attitude of gratitude to enhance positivity.

- Write three things you are grateful for each day.
- Reflect on why you are grateful for these things.
- When you're feeling down, remind yourself of the positives in your life.

I am Grateful for...

I am Grateful for...

I am Grateful for...

Practice Positive Self-Talk

Positive self-talk is like having a friendly cheerleader inside your head. It's about being kind and supportive to yourself, just like you would to a close friend. Instead of saying negative things like "I'm not good enough" or "I can't do it," positive self-talk helps us focus on the positive aspects of ourselves and our abilities.

Imagine you have a big test coming up, and you start feeling nervous. Negative self-talk might say, "I'm going to fail for sure." But with positive self-talk, you could tell yourself, "I've studied hard, and I'm prepared. I can do this!" See how that changes your mindset? It boosts your confidence and gives you a positive outlook.

Positive self-talk isn't about ignoring challenges or pretending everything is perfect. It's about approaching those challenges with a positive attitude. When faced with a difficult situation or a setback, you can say instead of beating yourself up, "It's okay; everyone makes mistakes. I'll learn from this and do better next time."

When you practice positive self-talk, you'll build self-belief and resilience. It helps you silence the negative voice that holds you back and replaces it with a positive and empowering one. You'll feel more confident in your abilities, which can improve your performance in various areas of life, such as academics, sports, or even personal relationships.

So how can you start practicing positive self-talk? It's all about awareness and consciously changing your thoughts. Pay attention to the negative self-talk that creeps into your mind. When you think negatively, pause and reframe it into something positive. It might feel strange initially, but the easier you do it, the easier it becomes.

 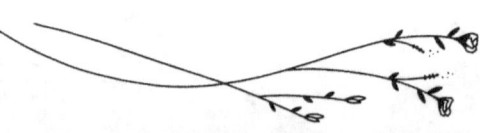

Also, surround yourself with positive influences. Spend time with supportive friends and family members who lift and encourage you. Engage in activities you enjoy and that make you feel good about yourself. Remember to celebrate your successes, no matter how small they may seem. Acknowledge your strengths and focus on your progress.

Practicing positive self-talk takes time and effort, but it can improve your life. Be kind to yourself, believe in your abilities, and embrace the awesome person that you are.

I speak to myself with kindness and positivity

Activity 3:
Cultivating Positive Self-Talk

The objective is to develop positive and compassionate self-talk habits.

- Write as much positive affirmations about yourself.
- Practice saying these affirmations out loud every morning and evening.
- Reflect on how your self-talk affects your mood and overall mindset.

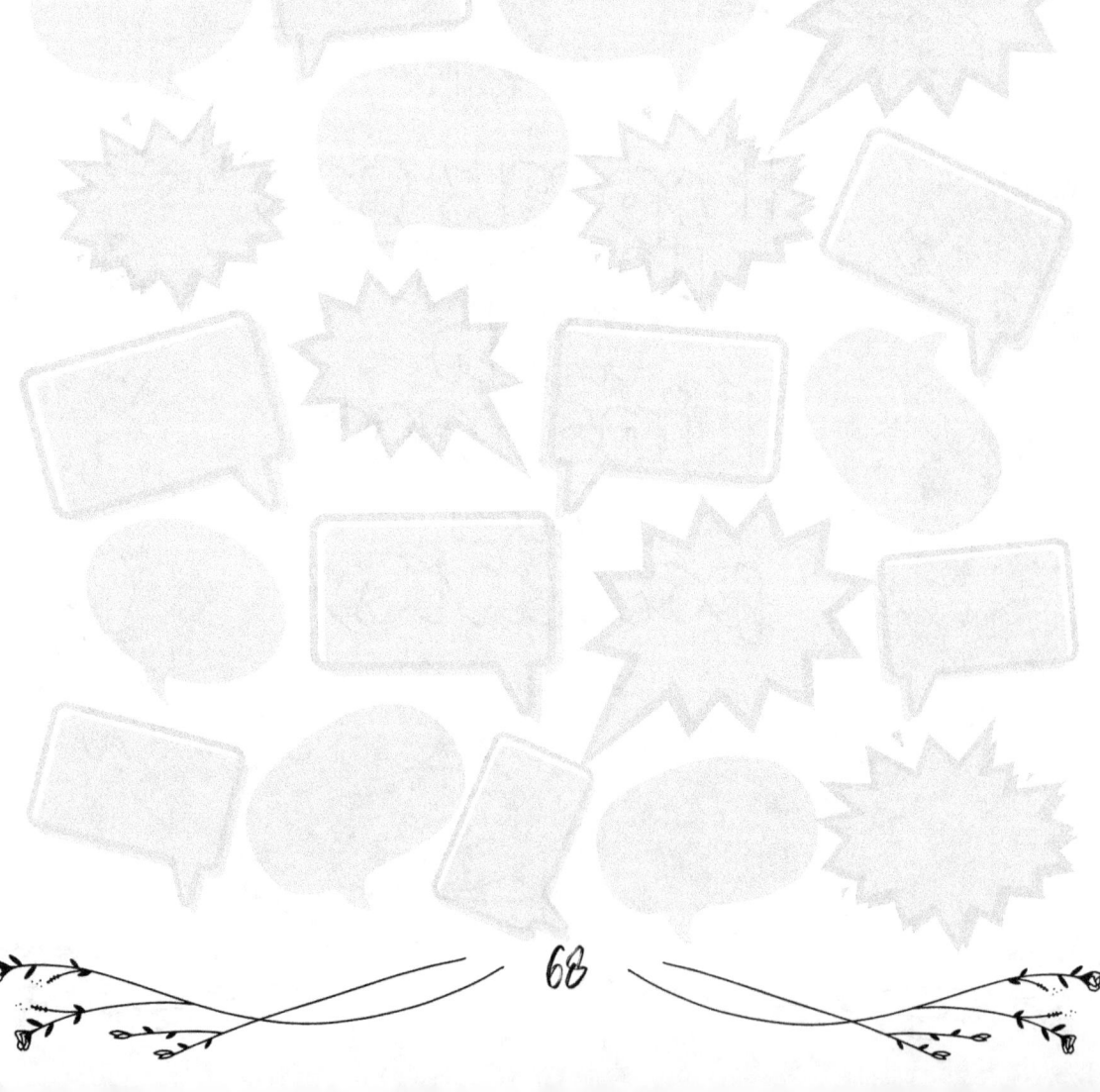

Activity 4: Embracing Affirmations

The objective is to utilize affirmations to promote positive thinking.

- Choose three affirmations that resonate with you.
- Write them down inside a frame and place them in prominent places (e.g., bedroom mirror, phone wallpaper) as reminders.
- Repeat your chosen affirmations several times daily, visualizing their positive impact on your life.

I am worthy and loved

This page was intentionally left blank

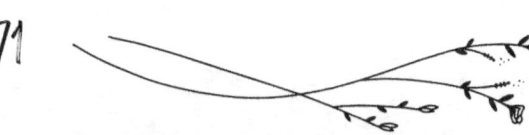

This page was intentionally left blank

This page was intentionally left blank

This page was intentionally left blank

Activity 5:
Building a Support System

The objective is to surround yourself with positive influences.

- Identify individuals who support and uplift you and write down their names.
- Reach out to them and express your gratitude for their positive impact.
- Limit contact with people who consistently bring negativity into your life.
- Engage in activities or join communities where you can connect with like-minded individuals.

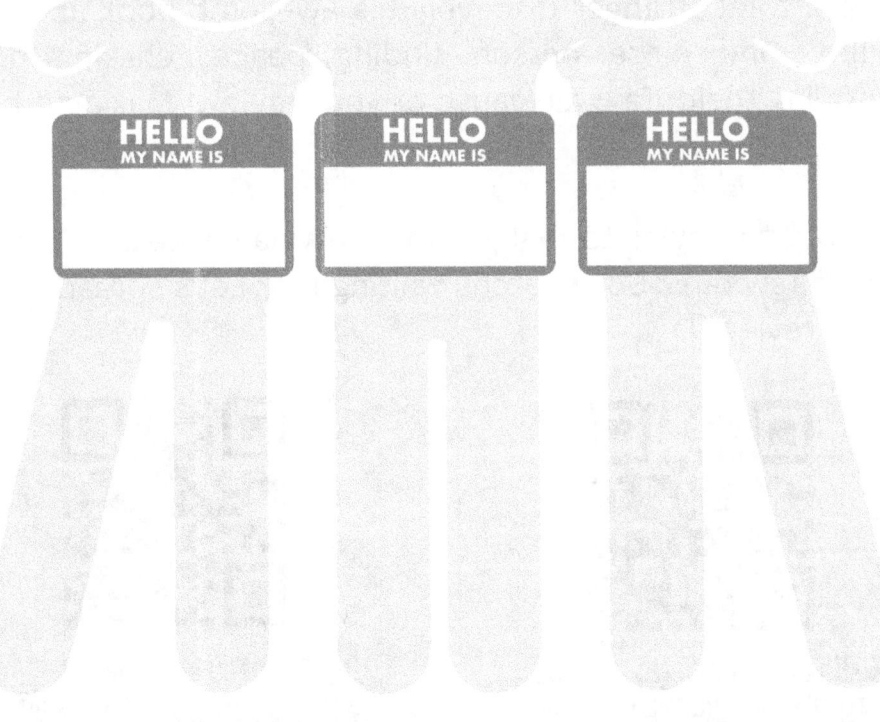

HELLO MY NAME IS

HELLO MY NAME IS

HELLO MY NAME IS

Helping Others

Hey there, Did you know? Being a helper without expecting anything back, boosts your happiness and success levels.(yep, seriously!).

If doing a good deed didn't cost a dime, would you help a stranger like a superhero without a cape? I've got a quick favor to ask.

At OBIEZ Publishing, we're all about helping folks on their journey, but we need to reach 'em first. And guess what? Reviews are golden tickets. So, if you feel this book could help another teenager, can you do something super quick?

Ready? Your honest review means the world. Seriously, it costs zero bucks and less than 60 seconds. But here's the magic: Your review will help a total stranger discover this awesome book and change their life. One more person finding peace, chasing dreams, transforming their life – all 'cause of your review! Making it happen is easy peasy!

You've got the power to make someone's day, week, or life better with just a few taps. So, whatcha waiting for? Let's spread the good vibes and reviews!

OBIEZ.COM/REVIEWSLWT
GO TO THE LINK ABOVE OR SCAN TO
LEAVE A REVIEW ON AMAZON **US**

OBIEZ.COM/REVIEWSLWT-UK
GO TO THE LINK ABOVE OR SCAN TO
LEAVE A REVIEW ON AMAZON **UK**

Chapter 4:
Unlock A Rock-Solid Mindset

Being a teenager can feel challenging. Your body is changing, your emotions are all over the place, and those crazy hormones can make everything even more confusing. It's normal to struggle with confidence and resilience during this time.

Meanwhile, having a rock-solid mindset can make a world of difference. It means your mind is strong, steady, and unshakable, like a sturdy rock. It's all about training your brain to think positively, stay focused, and believe in yourself no matter what.

With a rock-solid mindset, you can concentrate on your goals and dreams instead of getting stuck in negative thoughts. It helps you realize that tough times are temporary and won't stop you from achieving success.

The Importance of Having A Rock-Solid Mindset

A rock-solid mindset is essential because it affects how you see yourself and the world around you. When you have a positive mindset, you believe in your abilities and know you can handle whatever comes your way. This helps build confidence and self-esteem, which are crucial for personal growth and success.

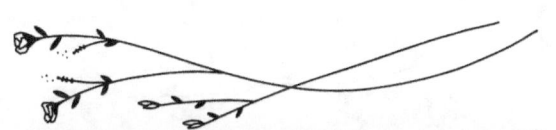 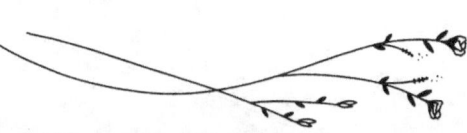

Life has ups and downs, and a rock-solid mindset helps you navigate challenging times. It's like having an anchor that keeps you grounded during storms. When faced with obstacles, you approach them with determination and a can-do attitude instead of getting discouraged or giving up. This mindset allows you to turn challenges into opportunities for growth and learning.

Another great thing about a rock-solid mindset is that it helps you develop resilience. Resilience means bouncing back from setbacks and not letting failures define you. It's about learning from your mistakes and using them as stepping stones to accomplish your goals. With a rock-solid mindset, you understand that failure is not the end but rather a chance to try again, smarter and stronger.

Your mindset also affects how you perceive and handle criticism. When you have a rock-solid mindset, you're open to feedback and see it as a chance to improve. You don't take criticism personally or let it bring you down. Instead, you use it as a tool for self-improvement and growth.

Having a positive mindset also helps you maintain a healthy outlook on life. It allows you to focus on the things you can control and not get overwhelmed by things you can't. It helps you develop a sense of gratitude for the good things in your life and find joy in the little moments.

However, having a rock-solid mindset doesn't mean you'll never have negative thoughts or challenging times. It's about building a mental foundation that helps you stay strong and optimistic, even when things get challenging. It's like having an inner cheerleader that encourages you to keep going and believe in yourself.

 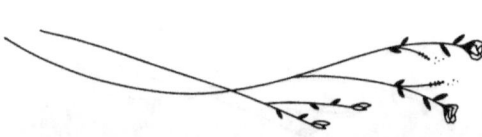

Differentiating Between Growth And Fixed Mindset

Imagine you're faced with a challenge or a difficult task. If you have a fixed mindset, you might think, "I can't do this; I'm just not good at it." You believe that your abilities and intelligence are fixed or set in stone. So when things get tough, you give up easily because you think there's no point in trying harder. It's like hitting a roadblock and feeling stuck.

On the other hand, having a growth mindset means believing that your abilities can be developed and improved through hard work, practice, and learning from mistakes. You understand that your intelligence and talents can be developed over time. So when faced with a challenge, you might think, "I may not be able to do it yet, but with effort and perseverance, I can learn and improve." It's like seeing obstacles as opportunities to learn and grow.

A growth mindset is essential because it helps you embrace challenges and view failures as stepping stones to success. With a growth mindset, you see effort as a positive thing and understand that it's the key to personal growth.

When you have a fixed mindset, you easily avoid challenges because you're afraid of failing and looking bad. But remember, failure is a natural part of learning and growing. It's how we figure out what works and what doesn't. When you have a growth mindset, you see failure as an opportunity to learn and improve. Instead of giving up, you keep going and try different strategies until you succeed.

 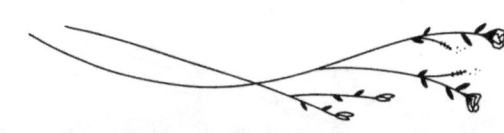

A growth mindset also means appreciating and learning from other people's success. Instead of feeling jealous or threatened, you see them as inspiration and learn from their achievements. You believe that if they can do it, you can, too, with the right mindset and effort.

So, the key difference between a growth mindset and a fixed mindset is how you view your abilities and approach challenges. A growth mindset is about believing in your potential to learn and improve. In contrast, a fixed mindset holds you back by making you believe your abilities are fixed and unchangeable.

It's normal to sometimes slip into a fixed mindset, but the important thing is to catch yourself and try to shift back to a growth mindset. With a growth mindset, you can overcome obstacles, reach your goals, and become the best version of yourself.

Boost Your Self-Esteem And Confidence

Boosting your self-esteem and confidence is vital during your teenage years when figuring out who you are and navigating through all kinds of experiences. But how can you do this?

First, embracing and accepting yourself just as you are is essential. You're unique and special, with strengths, talents, and quirks that make you who you are. Embracing your individuality and being proud of yourself is the first step toward building confidence.

Next, it's essential to set realistic goals for yourself. Setting achievable goals allows you to see your progress and celebrate your accomplishments. Whether it's acing a test, learning a new skill, or improving your fitness, each step forward boosts your confidence and makes you feel more capable.

Meanwhile, it's okay to make mistakes. We all do! Instead of beating yourself up over them, learn from them. Mistakes are opportunities for growth and learning. When you adopt a positive mindset and view challenges as stepping stones, you'll build resilience and feel more confident handling whatever comes your way.

Another tip is to surround yourself with positive people who uplift and support you. Choose friends who appreciate and value you for who you are. Positive friendships can do wonders for your self-esteem. And remember, it's crucial to be a good friend yourself too! Supporting others will also make you feel good about yourself.

Avoid comparing yourself to others. It's easy to fall into the trap of comparing yourself to others, especially with the rise of social media. Remember that everyone has their journey and struggles. Focus on your progress and achievements instead of comparing them to someone else's. Embrace your unique path and be proud of your accomplishments.

Lastly, practice self-care and self-love. Treat yourself with kindness, compassion, and respect. Celebrate your strengths and achievements, no matter how small they may seem. Take time for activities that make you happy and help you relax. When you prioritize self-care and show love to yourself, your self-esteem will soar.

How To Be Resilient Even In Tough Times

Life can be challenging, but you have the strength to overcome it and become resilient. Being resilient means bouncing back from difficult situations and finding the courage to keep going. Here are some tips to help you build resilience:

- Accept and acknowledge your feelings.

Feeling upset, frustrated, or sad when things aren't going well is okay. Accepting your emotions is the first step in dealing with them. Don't be too hard on yourself for feeling a certain way.

- Reach out for support.

You don't have to face tough times alone. Reach out to friends, family, or a trusted adult. Please share your thoughts and feelings with them, and don't be afraid to ask for help or advice.

- Practice positive thinking.

It's easy to get caught up in negative thoughts during tough times. Try to change your mindset and focus on the positive aspects of your life. Surround yourself with positivity, whether it's through uplifting music, inspiring quotes, or spending time with supportive friends.

- Learn from setbacks.

Mistakes and setbacks are part of life and can teach us valuable lessons. Instead of dwelling on failures, try to see them as opportunities for growth and learning. Take a moment to reflect on what went wrong, what you could have done differently, and what you have learned from it.

- Keep a long-term perspective.

Tough times are temporary. Visualize the future you want for yourself and focus on the steps you need to take to get there. Keeping a long-term perspective can give you hope and motivation to keep pushing forward.

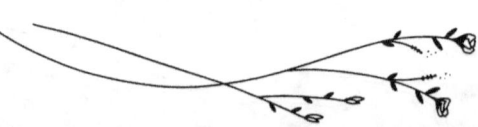

How to Foster a Growth Mindset

A growth mindset means a conviction that your abilities can be developed through practice and effort. It's all about embracing challenges, learning from failures, and seeing setbacks as opportunities for growth. So, let's dive into some practical tips on how you can cultivate a growth mindset:

- Embrace Challenges.
Instead of avoiding challenges, face them head-on! Challenges help you learn and grow. Remember, it's okay to make mistakes because they are a natural part of the learning process.

- Change "I Can't" to "I Can't Yet."
When you feel stuck or face a difficult task, shift your mindset by adding "yet" to your thoughts. For example, instead of saying, "I can't solve this math problem," say, "I can't solve this math problem yet." It keeps you focused on the idea that you can improve with time and effort.

- See Failure as a Learning Opportunity.
Failure is not the end of the road; it's a chance to learn and improve. When you encounter failure, ask yourself, "What can I learn from this?" Analyze what went wrong, adjust your approach, and try again. Remember, successful people have often failed multiple times before achieving greatness.

- Emphasize Effort and Hard Work
Instead of focusing solely on natural talent or intelligence, value the effort you put into your goals. Recognize that hard work and dedication are the keys to success. Celebrate your progress and achievements, no matter how small they may seem.

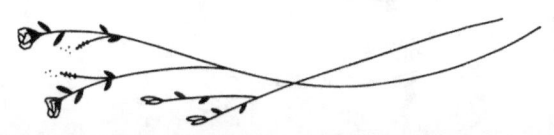
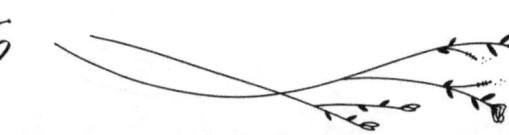

- Take Risks.

Leaving your comfort zone is essential for personal growth. Trying new things, whether joining a club, learning a new skill, or pursuing a passion, allows you to discover your interests and talents. Don't fear failure or judgment; remember that growth happens outside your comfort zone.

- Practice Self-Reflection.

Take time to reflect on your progress, strengths, and areas where you can improve. Set realistic goals and break them down into smaller, manageable steps. Celebrate each milestone you achieve, and adjust your plans as needed.

- Be Kind to Yourself.

Developing a growth mindset involves being kind and compassionate to yourself. Don't be too hard on yourself when you face setbacks or make mistakes. Treat yourself with the same patience and understanding you would offer a friend.

I believe in my potential to improve. Every step forward is a victory

Activity 1:
Embracing Challenges

The objective is to understand the importance of challenges in personal growth.

- Read the following quote by Joshua J. Marine aloud and reflect on its meaning
- Share an example of a recent challenge and how you overcame. Explain why this challenge was necessary for your personal growth.

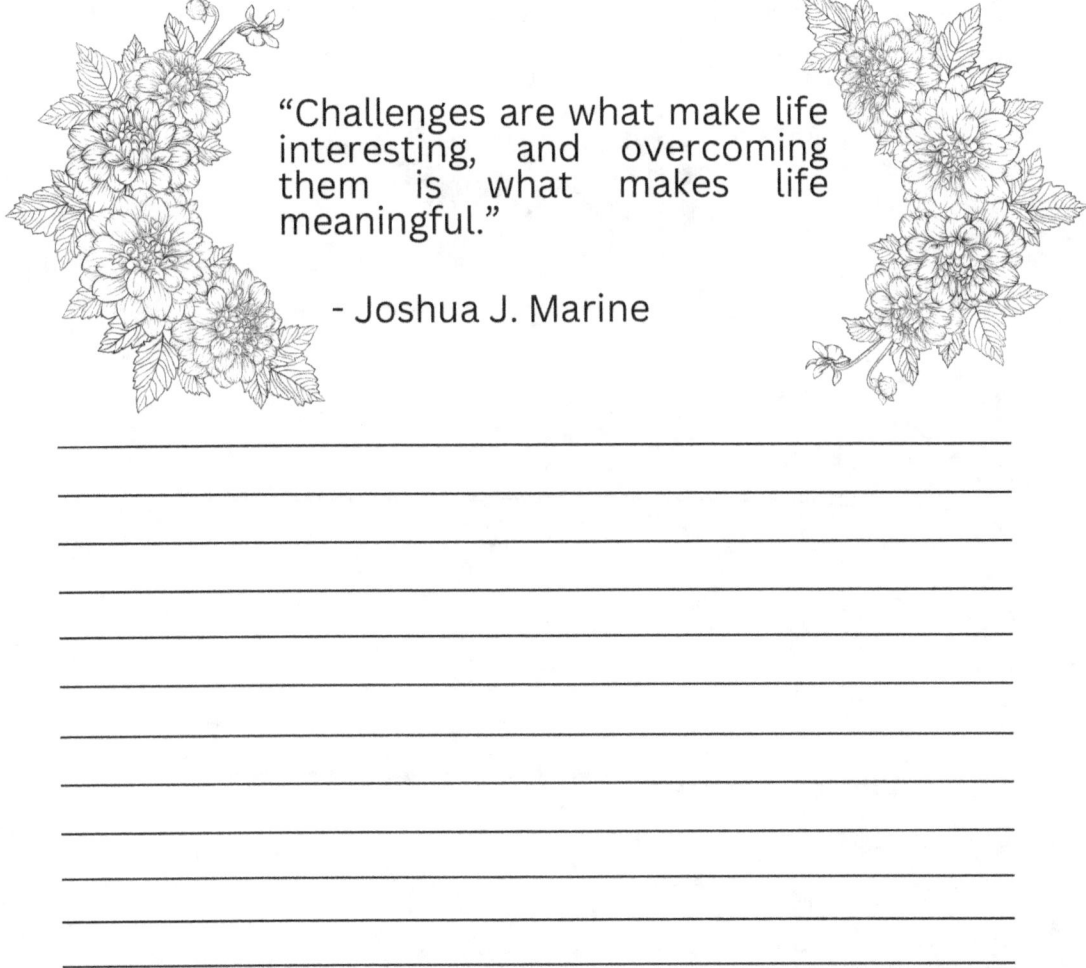

"Challenges are what make life interesting, and overcoming them is what makes life meaningful."

- Joshua J. Marine

_____
_____
_____
_____
_____
_____
_____
_____
_____
_____
_____
_____
_____

Activity 2:
The Power of Yet

The objective is to develop a positive outlook toward learning and improvement.

- Write down three goals or skills you would like to improve. Read them aloud and remind yourself that you still need to achieve them. Embrace the power of yet, knowing that with effort and dedication, you can accomplish anything.
- Share one of your goals with a friend, family member, or mentor. Discuss how you plan to work towards it and seek their support and encouragement.

My Goals

1.

_____

2.

_____

3.

Activity 3:
Positive Self-Talk

The objective is to cultivate self-compassion and positive self-beliefs.

- Think about a recent setback or mistake.
- Rewrite the negative self-talk associated with it into positive and constructive statements.
- Make a list of positive affirmations about yourself.
- Read them aloud, emphasizing each word to boost your confidence and self-belief.

Activity 4:
Learning from Failure

The objective is to reframe failure as an opportunity for growth.
- Recall a recent failure or disappointment. Read aloud the following questions and take time to reflect on them
- Share your reflections with a peer or mentor, discussing the lessons learned and strategies for bouncing back stronger.

What can I learn from this experience?

_____
_____
_____
_____
_____

How can I use this setback as a stepping stone for future success?

_____
_____
_____
_____
_____

How can I improve and do better next time?

_____
_____
_____
_____
_____

Activity 5:
Cultivating Resilience

The objective is to develop resilience in the face of challenges.

- Read aloud the story of a famous person who faced numerous challenges but overcame them through resilience (e.g., Oprah Winfrey, Malala Yousafzai, Serena Williams).

What qualities they demonstrated on their journey?

_____

_____

_____

_____

_____

Write 3 strategies you learned that you can use to build resilience in your own life?

_____

_____

_____

_____

_____

_____

- Share your ideas with someone you trust and discuss how they can support you in developing resilience.

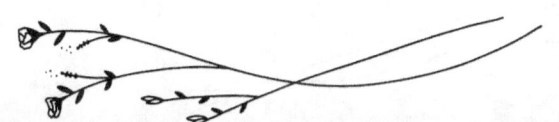 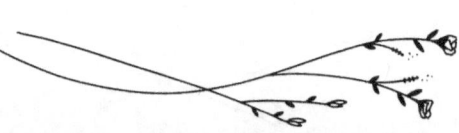

Chapter 5:
Fill Your Cup With Self-Care

Like plugging your phone or any other device to let it recharge, your body and mind work the same way.

Sometimes we all feel tired and worn out, and that's completely normal. It can happen because of physical pain, feeling sad or anxious, being stressed out, having a lot on your plate, taking care of others, or going through a tough time like losing someone you love. This is why taking care of yourself is crucial for your well-being.

So, what exactly is self-care? It's all about doing things that make you feel mentally and physically good. It's like giving yourself a little treat or a break to recharge your batteries. Self-care helps you have the energy you need to handle the challenges of everyday life.

The important thing is to make self-care a priority in your life. You should not feel guilty about or think you don't deserve it. Taking care of yourself is essential; you deserve to feel happy and well. So, let's explore some aspects of self-care you should embrace.

Physical

Physical self-care is all about caring for your body, inside and out, so you can feel good and stay healthy. It's simply giving yourself a little pampering session and showing your body some love.

There are many ways you can practice physical self-care. Let's start with the basics: hygiene. Regular showers or baths, washing your hair, brushing your teeth, and wearing clean clothes are all essential for keeping yourself clean and fresh. It might sound simple, but these everyday habits make a big difference in how you feel and how others perceive you.

Now, let's move on to some fun stuff! Taking care of your skin is a great way to practice physical self-care. This means washing your face daily to keep it clean and using a moisturizer to keep it soft and hydrated. If you're into makeup, remember to remove it before bed to let your skin breathe and prevent breakouts.

Exercise is another essential aspect of physical self-care. Find activities you enjoy, whether dancing, swimming, running, or playing a sport. Regular exercise helps you stay fit, boosts your mood, and increases your energy levels. Plus, it's a great way to meet new friends if you join a sports team or a dance class!

Taking care of your diet is also part of physical self-care. Eat a balanced diet with whole grains, plenty of vegetables, fruits, and lean proteins. It's okay to indulge in some treats occasionally, but moderation is key.

Getting adequate sleep is beneficial for your physical and mental health. Your body is still growing and developing as a teenager, so aim for 8-9 hours of sleep each night. It helps your body recharge, improves your concentration, and keeps your mood in check.

Lastly, remember relaxation and stress management. Life can get hectic, so finding ways to unwind and care for your mental health is crucial. This could be anything from reading a book, listening to music, practicing mindfulness or meditation, or engaging in a hobby you love.

Physical self-care is about nurturing your body, staying healthy, and feeling good about yourself. It's not about looking a certain way or comparing yourself to others. It's about embracing your unique qualities and caring for yourself because you deserve it!

Activity 1:
Nourish Your Body

Balanced Bites:

- Create a meal plan for a day that includes foods from each food group.
- Include healthy and delicious snack options in your daily routine.

	Breakfast	Lunch	Dinner
Monday			
Tuesday			
Wednesday			
Thursday			
Friday			
Saturday			
Sunday			

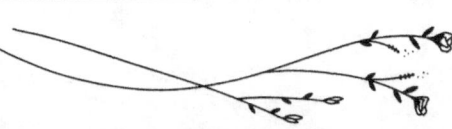

Activity 2:
Move Your Body

Energize and Exercise:
- Create a personalized exercise routine incorporating activities you enjoy (e.g., dancing, yoga, jogging).
- Set goals for physical activity and track your progress over a month.

Mindful Movement:
- Practice mindful exercises, such as deep breathing or stretching, to release tension and improve focus.
- Design your workout playlist to enhance your exercise experience.

Get Active Outdoors:
- Explore nature by planning outdoor activities like hiking, biking, or swimming.
- Share a photo or drawing of your favorite outdoor adventure and describe how it made you feel.

Move Your Body

MOTHLY PLANNER

MONTH............... YEAR...............

1	**2**	**3**	**4**	**5**
6	**7**	**8**	**9**	**10**
11	**12**	**13**	**14**	**15**
16	**17**	**18**	**19**	**20**
21	**22**	**23**	**24**	**25**
26	**27**	**28**	**29**	**30**

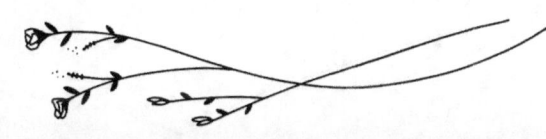
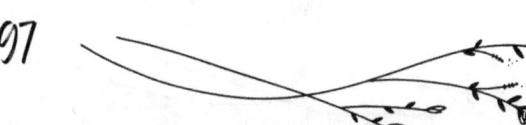

97

Activity 3:
Pamper Your Skin

Daily Skincare Routine:
- Create a step-by-step skincare routine that suits your skin type.
- Research natural ingredients and their benefits for healthy skin.

MORNING

NIGHT

STEP 1

STEP 2

STEP 3

STEP 4

STEP 5

STEP 6

STEP 7

DIY Spa Day

Plan a relaxing spa day at home with homemade facemasks, body scrubs, or a soothing bath.
Write a journal entry about your spa day experience and its positive effects on your well-being.

Face

Hair

Body

Mood

Hands

Feet

Activity 4:
Self-Expression

Fashion Forward:

- Experiment with different styles and create a lookbook showcasing your favorite outfits.

- Write a short paragraph describing how fashion allows you to express your unique personality.

_____
_____
_____
_____
_____
_____
_____
_____
_____
_____
_____
_____
_____
_____
_____
_____
_____
_____
_____
_____
_____
_____

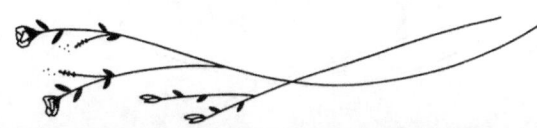 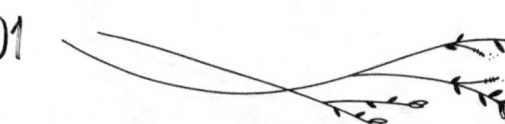

Creative Expression

- Engage in creative activities like writing, drawing, or painting to express emotions.
- Share your creation with someone and describe the feelings it evokes.

Emotional

Emotional self-care entails caring for your emotions and ensuring you're in an excellent mental and emotional state. It's like giving yourself a big, warm hug from the inside.

You know those days when you feel overwhelmed, stressed, or just not quite yourself? Emotional self-care is like a superpower that helps you deal with those feelings and take steps to feel better.
So, how do you practice emotional self-care? Here are a few ideas:

- Embrace Challenges.

It's essential to be aware of how you're feeling. Are you sad, anxious, angry, or happy? Take a moment to check in with yourself and give your emotions some attention. It's okay to feel whatever you're feeling.

- Find healthy ways to express your emotions.

It would help to express your emotions instead of bottling them up inside. You can practice journaling, talk to a friend or family member, or even create art to express those feelings.

- Take time for yourself.

Permit yourself to take breaks and do things you enjoy. It could be reading a book, listening to music, walking, or practicing a hobby. Taking time for yourself allows you to recharge and relax.

Set boundaries: It's important to set limits and say no when necessary. You don't have to do everything or please everyone. It's okay to prioritize your needs and take care of yourself first.

Meanwhile, emotional self-care is a journey that differs for everyone. You should try different strategies to find the best for you. So, be patient with yourself, and don't hesitate to ask for help if you need it.

Activity 5:
Understanding Your Emotions

- Start an emotion journal to track and explore your emotions daily.
- Write down the emotions you experienced, what caused them, and how you responded.
- Reflect on patterns or recurring emotions and any shifts in your emotional well-being.

what emotions did you experienced?

_____
_____
_____

what caused them?

_____
_____
_____

How did you respond?

_____
_____
_____

Did you notice any patterns or recurring emotion?

_____
_____
_____

Activity 6:
Expressing Your Emotions

- Choose a specific emotion you're currently experiencing.
- Write a letter to that emotion, expressing your thoughts, feelings, and concerns.
- Reflect on the insights gained through this exercise and any relief experienced.

Dear_____:

_____

_____

_____

_____

_____

_____

_____

_____

Reflextions

Activity 7:
Nurturing Your Emotions

- Write down three positive affirmations about yourself and your emotions.
- Practice self-compassion by speaking these affirmations aloud every day.
- Reflect on how this exercise impacts your self-image and emotional well-being.

I AM...

I AM...

I AM...

Activity 8:
Gratitude Jar

- Every day write down in your jar things that you're grateful for.
- Keep filling your jar with gratitude until it is overflowing with gratitude, then start a new jar.
- Reflect on how focusing on gratitude impacts your overall mood and emotional resilience.
- Challenge yourself to find new things to appreciate, even in difficult situations.

Spiritual

Spiritual self-care focuses on nurturing your inner self and finding purpose and peace. It's all about caring for your spirit or soul, just like you would take care of your body and mind.

Your spiritual self is like a beautiful garden that needs attention and care to flourish. When you practice spiritual self-care, you're tending to that garden and helping it grow.

So, how can you do that? There are many ways to nurture your spiritual self, and it's all about finding what resonates with you. Here are a few ideas:

- Reflection and mindfulness
Take some time to be still and quiet. Meditate, journal, or sit peacefully and let your thoughts flow. It helps you become more aware of your emotions, thoughts, and world.

- Connecting with nature
Spend time outdoors and soak up the beauty of nature. Walking in the park, hiking in the woods, or simply sitting under a tree, being in nature, can be calming and grounding. It helps you appreciate the world's wonders and feel connected to something greater.

- Gratitude practice
Cultivate a grateful mindset by focusing on the positive things in your life. Consider what you're grateful for each day, whether it's your family, friends, a sunny day, or even a delicious meal. It shifts your perspective and brings more joy and contentment into your life.

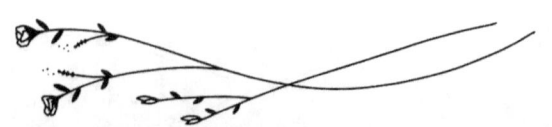 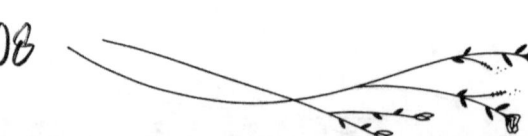

- Engage in creative activities.

Find an artistic outlet that sparks joy in you. It could be painting, playing an instrument, writing, dancing, or self-expression. Creativity allows you to tap into your inner thoughts and feelings, which can be incredibly fulfilling.

- Seek wisdom and inspiration.

Listen to podcasts, read books, or watch videos that inspire and uplift you. Explore different philosophies, spiritual practices, or teachings that resonate with you. It broadens your perspective and helps you grow intellectually and spiritually.

Spiritual self-care is a personal journey, and there's no right or wrong way to do it. It's about finding what brings you peace, joy, and a deeper understanding of yourself and the world around you.

I listen to the whispers of my heart, finding joy and comfort in the beauty of my soul

Activity 9:
Setting Intentions

- Take a few deep breaths and create a calm and peaceful environment around you.
- Reflect on your spiritual state and set your intentions for using this workbook.
- What areas of your spiritual life do you want to focus on?
- Write down your intentions and keep them in mind as you progress through the activities.

Activity 10:
Mindful Meditation

1 Find a quiet space where you can sit comfortably.

2 Close your eyes and focus on your breath.

3 Take slow and deep breaths, Imagine positivity and peace flowing into your body as you inhale

4 Release any tension or negative thoughts as you exhale.

5 After a while, expand awareness to sounds, sensations, and surroundings without attachment or aversion.

6 when ready, open your eyes slowly. Notice how you feel after meditation. Carry this mindfulness with you throughout your day.

7 Practice mindful meditation for a few minutes daily to connect with your inner self.

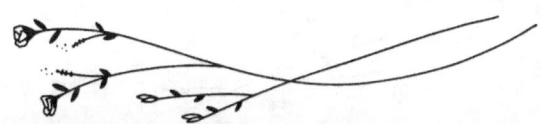 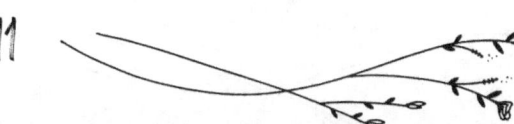

Mindful Meditation Journal

- Keep a log of your mindfulness meditation sessions.
- Note how you were feeling before starting and after finishing.
- Reflect on your emotions and experiences during the practice.

Date & Time: _____ Duration:_____
Feeling before: _____
_____
Feeling after: _____
_____

Date & Time: _____ Duration:_____
Feeling before: _____
_____
Feeling after: _____
_____

Date & Time: _____ Duration:_____
Feeling before: _____
_____
Feeling after: _____
_____

Date & Time: _____ Duration:_____
Feeling before: _____
_____
Feeling after: _____
_____

Date & Time: _____ Duration:_____
Feeling before: _____
_____
Feeling after: _____
_____

Date & Time: _____ Duration:_____
Feeling before: _____
_____
Feeling after: _____
_____

Date & Time: _____ Duration:_____
Feeling before: _____
_____
Feeling after: _____
_____

Date & Time: _____ Duration:_____
Feeling before: _____
_____
Feeling after: _____
_____

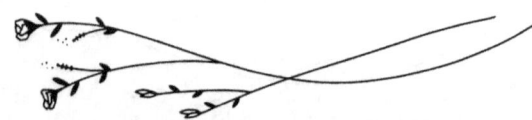 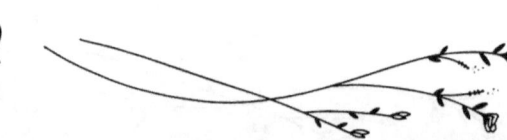

Activity 11: Nature Walk

1 Go for a walk in nature and pay attention to your surroundings

2 Observe the colors, textures, sounds, and smells around you.

3 Connect with the natural world and feel the peace it brings

4 Reflect on the beauty of nature and how it makes you feel.

5 Take pictures or write down your thoughts in a journal to capture these moments.

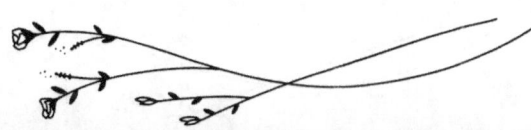 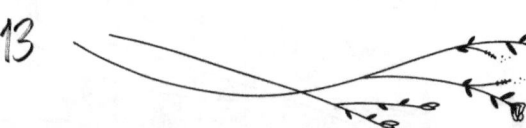

Nature Walk Photo Album

Activity 12:
Journaling Prompts

Use the following prompts to explore your thoughts and emotions:

What does spirituality mean to you?

_____
_____
_____

What spiritual practices or rituals resonate with you?

_____
_____
_____

How do you find meaning and purpose in life?

_____
_____
_____

Describe a time when you felt deeply connected to something greater than yourself.

_____
_____
_____

What role does compassion play in your spiritual journey?

_____
_____
_____

Activity 13:
Acts of Kindness

- Perform acts of kindness to spread positivity and love.
- Volunteer at a local charity, help a friend in need or engage in random acts of kindness for strangers.
- Reflect on how these acts make you feel and their impact on others. Remember, small acts of kindness can have a big ripple effect.

How did you make a difference?

_____
_____
_____
_____

How did it make you feel?

_____
_____
_____
_____

What did you learn?

_____
_____
_____
_____

Psychological

Psychological self-care involves doing activities and practicing habits that make you feel good and help you cope with the ups and downs of life. It's like giving yourself a mental recharge. Just like you might enjoy painting, playing video games, or spending time with friends, psychological self-care is about finding things that bring you joy, peace, and a sense of fulfillment.

One way to take care of your psychological well-being is by practicing self-awareness. This means paying attention to your thoughts, emotions, and feelings in different situations. By being aware of your mind and emotions, you can better understand yourself and make good choices.

Another important aspect of psychological self-care is managing stress. Life can be pretty hectic, and stress can build up. It's essential to find healthy ways to deal with stress. You can try deep breathing exercises, meditation, journaling, or even talking to someone you trust about what's bothering you. Remember, it's okay to ask for help when you need it.

Additionally, finding activities that help you relax and recharge is crucial. It could be reading a book, walking in nature, practicing a hobby, or listening to music. Whatever makes you feel calm and happy, make time for it regularly.

Activity 14:
Explore your thoughts and emotions through reflective writing.

- Set aside time daily to journal your experiences, emotions, and challenges.

What happened?

_____
_____
_____

What did you feel?

_____
_____
_____

What did you think?

_____
_____
_____

What did you learn?

_____
_____
_____
_____

Activity 15:
Foster meaningful relationships and connect with others

- Identify who are you circle of support that you would like to work on a meaningful relationship
- Contact them and plan a get-together.
- Practice active listening skills when communicating with others, showing empathy and understanding.
- Create your

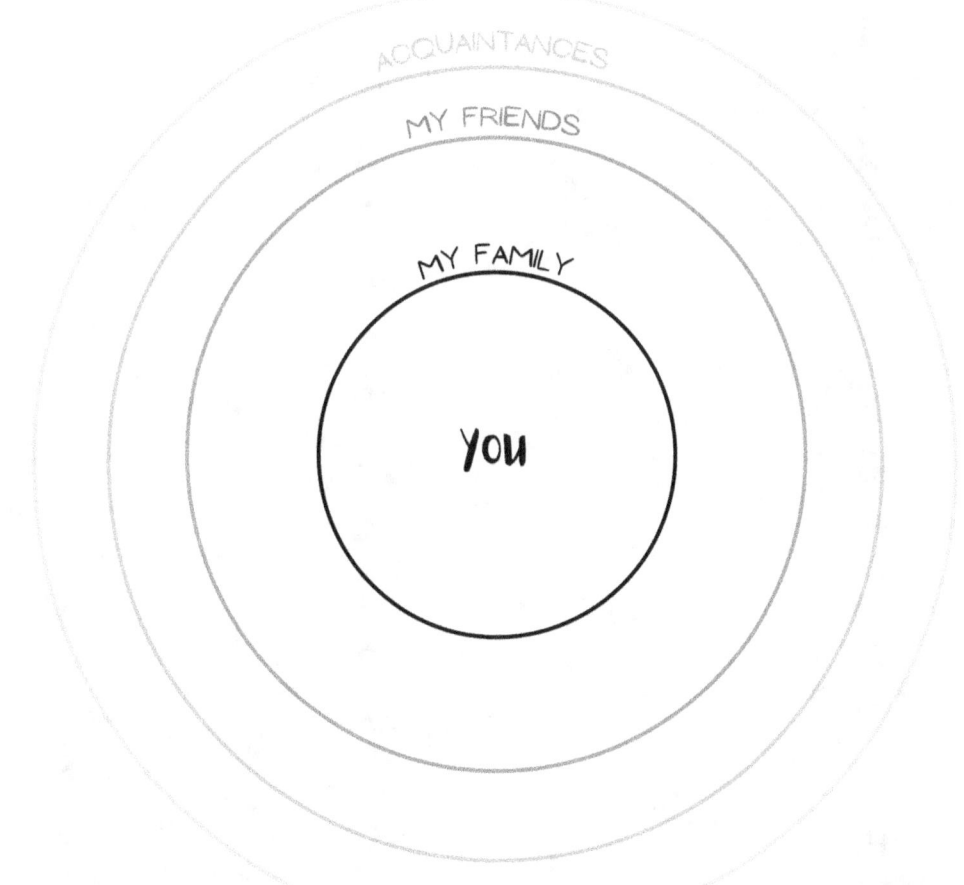

Activity 16:
Take a break from technology to prioritize self-care.

- Designate specific "tech-free" periods during the day and engage in offline activities.
- Create a list of alternative activities when you want to reach for your phone or computer.
- Explore outdoor activities like hiking, gardening, or playing a sport to disconnect and reconnect with nature.

Tech Free Activities!

1	16
2	17
3	18
4	19
5	20
6	21
7	22
8	23
9	24
10	25
11	26
12	27
13	28
14	29
15	30

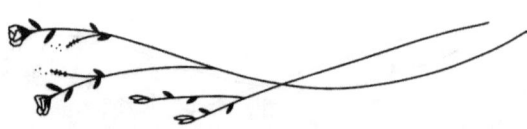
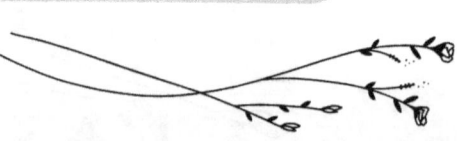

Activity 17:
Self-Care Plan

- List three self-care activities that bring joy and help you cope with difficult emotions. For example: taking a bubble bath, walking in nature, practicing yoga, etc.
- Commit to doing at least one of these self-care activities each day for the next week. Notice how it impacts your overall well-being.

Conclusion

Well done, girl!

I commend you for staying with me throughout this journey – you've done an excellent job!

As a teenager, you've been overwhelmed with multiple levels by comparisons, relationship issues, school concerns, and even personal attacks. Unlike in the past, where technology didn't add to the mix, the internet has created a dynamic where teens get little or no rest from social criticism, making it hard to practice self-love.

This workbook has tried to solve the issue by showing you different factors to self-love and how to improve your self-love and create a healthy mindset to carry you throughout your life!

The workbook has many simple activities you can work with in different settings. I believe you can work and journal through this workbook on your own.

So far, you've gained invaluable knowledge and can now start your journey to self-love.

If this book has impacted your life or has helped you in any way, kindly let other struggling teens know by dropping a review and sharing your experience.

Best wishes!

 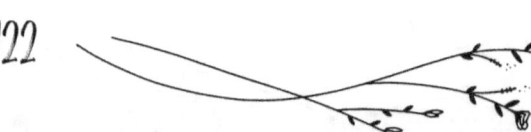

Thank you so much for supporting my dream as an independent author.

Your decision to purchase and read my book means everything to me!
I couldn't have made it this far without amazing readers like you!

As you know, reviews are crucial for independent authors like me to reach a wider audience and continue pursuing our passion.

I would greatly appreciate it if you could leave an honest review on Amazon by scanning the QR code below or going to the link below.

OBIEZ.COM/REVIEWSLWT
CLICK OR SCAN TO LEAVE A REVIEW
ON AMAZON **US**

OBIEZ.COM/REVIEWSLWT-UK
CLICK OR SCAN TO LEAVE A REVIEW
ON AMAZON **UK**

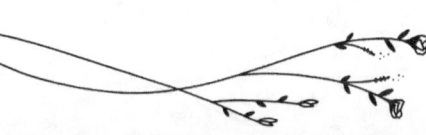

References

Beatanxiety. (n.d.). Common Self-Love Obstacles People Face. Retrieved from https://beatanxiety.me/common-self-love-obstacles-people-face/

Berkeley Well-Being Institute. (n.d.). Self-Love. Retrieved from https://www.berkeleywellbeing.com/self-love.html

Brene Brown. (2010). The Gifts of Imperfection: Let Go of Who You Think You're Supposed to Be and Embrace Who You Are. Hazelden Publishing.

Brown, B. (2012). Daring Greatly: How the Courage to Be Vulnerable Transforms the Way We Live, Love, Parent, and Lead. Gotham.

Chawla, T. (2021, March 22). 8 Ways to Practice Self-Love. Verywell Mind. Retrieved from https://www.verywellmind.com/ways-to-practice-self-love-5667417

Chopra, D. (1991). The Seven Spiritual Laws of Success: A Practical Guide to the Fulfillment of Your Dreams. Amber-Allen Publishing.

Dweck, C. S. (2007). Mindset: The New Psychology of Success. Ballantine Books.

Dweck, C. S. (2021). Carol Dweck's Mindset: The New Psychology of Success. Retrieved from https://mindsetonline.com/

Foundations Asheville. (n.d.). Self-Limiting Beliefs and Behaviors. Retrieved from https://foundationsasheville.com/blog/self-limiting-beliefs-and-behaviors/

Foundation for Psychiatric Research. (n.d.). Self-Love and What It Means. Brain & Behavior Research Foundation. Retrieved from https://www.bbrfoundation.org/blog/self-love-and-what-it-means#:~:text=Self%2Dlove%20means%20having%20a,for%20less%20than%20you%20deserve.

FutureLearn. (n.d.). 6 Tips to Develop a Growth Mindset. Retrieved from https://www.futurelearn.com/info/blog/general/develop-growth-mindset.

 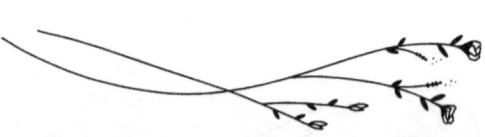

Germer, C. K. (2009). The Mindful Path to Self-Compassion: Freeing Yourself from Destructive Thoughts and Emotions. The Guilford Press.

Harvard Business School Online. (n.d.). Growth Mindset vs. Fixed Mindset. Retrieved from https://online.hbs.edu/blog/post/growth-mindset-vs-fixed-mindset#:~:text=Someone%20with%20a%20growth%20mindset,stable%20and%20unchangeable%20over%20time.

HelpGuide. (2021, June). Stress Management: Surviving Tough Times. Retrieved from https://www.helpguide.org/articles/stress/surviving-tough-times.htm

Hinge Health. (n.d.). Filling Your Cup: The Importance of Self-Care. Retrieved from https://www.hingehealth.com/resources/articles/filling-your-cup-the-importance-of-self-care/

Markert, K. (n.d.). How to Create a Rock-Solid Mindset: The Mindset Manifesto. Retrieved from https://medium.com/@kilianmarkert/how-to-create-a-rock-solid-mindset-the-mindset-manifesto-29308f57e0bb

Mayo Clinic Staff. (2020, July 14). Positive thinking: Stop negative self-talk to reduce stress. Mayo Clinic. Retrieved from https://www.mayoclinic.org/healthy-lifestyle/stress-management/in-depth/positive-thinking/art-20043950

Medical News Today. (2018, November 16). How to Learn Self Love. Retrieved from https://www.medicalnewstoday.com/articles/321309

Middle Earth. (2020, November 9). Helping Teens Develop Self-Awareness. Retrieved from https://middleearthnj.org/2020/11/09/helping-teens-develop-self-awareness/

 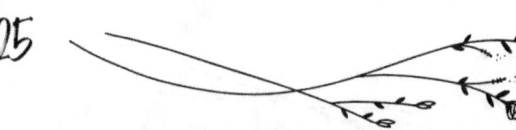

Narley K. (n.d.). 6 Barriers That Block You From Self-Love. Retrieved from https://www.narleyk.com/6-barriers-that-block-you-from-self-love/

Neff, K. D. (2003). Self-Compassion: An Alternative Conceptualization of a Healthy Attitude Toward Oneself. Self and Identity, 2(2), 85-101. DOI: 10.1080/15298860309032

Neff, K. (2021). The Official Self-Compassion Website. Retrieved from https://self-compassion.org/

Nordqvist, C. (2018, November 16). How to Learn Self Love. Medical News Today. Retrieved from https://www.medicalnewstoday.com/articles/321309

Positive Psychology. (n.d.). Emotion Regulation Worksheets & Strategies (DBT Skills). Retrieved from https://positivepsychology.com/emotion-regulation-worksheets-strategies-dbt-skills/

Rosenberg, M. (2015). Nonviolent Communication: A Language of Life. PuddleDancer Press.

Siegel, D. J. (2010). The Whole-Brain Child: 12 Revolutionary Strategies to Nurture Your Child's Developing Mind. Bantam.

Siegel, D. J. (2012). Mindsight: The New Science of Personal Transformation. Bantam.

Smith, M., Segal, J., & Segal, R. (2021, June). Stress Management: Surviving Tough Times. HelpGuide. Retrieved from https://www.helpguide.org/articles/stress/surviving-tough-times.htm

Smith, T. (2019, May 29). What Is Self-Love and Why Is It So Important? Psych Central. Retrieved from https://psychcentral.com/blog/imperfect/2019/05/what-is-self-love-and-why-is-it-so-important

Thich Nhat Hanh. (2010). The Miracle of Mindfulness: An Introduction to the Practice of Meditation. Beacon Press.

Williams, N. (n.d.). 4 Common Barriers to Self-Love. Retrieved from https://drnatashawilliams.com/4-common-barriers-to-self-love/

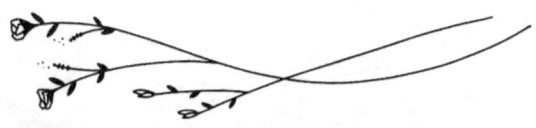 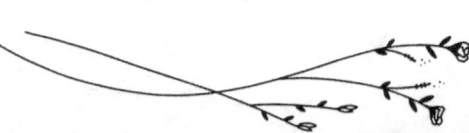

www.ingramcontent.com/pod-product-compliance
Lightning Source LLC
Chambersburg PA
CBHW082108120626
46553CB00011B/3591